SEEING IS BELIEVING

Visions of Life Through Film

Robert Benne

University Press of America,® Inc.
Lanham • New York • Oxford

Copyright © 1998
University Press of America,® Inc.
4720 Boston Way
Lanham, Maryland 20706

12 Hid's Copse Rd.
Cumnor Hill, Oxford OX2 9JJ

Library of Congress Cataloging-in-Publication Data

Benne, Robert
Seeing is believing : visions of life through film / Robert Benne.
p.   cm.
Includes bibliographical references.
1. Motion pictures—Religious aspects. 2. Motion pictures—
Evaluation. I. Title.
PN1995.9.R4B45   1998   791.43'682—dc21   98-30924 CIP

ISBN 0-7618-1268-7 (pbk: alk. ppr.)

Contents

Preface

This book is a tribute to the cliché that necessity is the mother of invention. I began teaching courses in film interpretation in the early 1970s. During the nearly thirty years since then I have searched for the text that would be helpful to me and the class in communicating the approach that I was developing. While some texts have moved in a preferred direction—the most recent being *Images and Likeness: Religious Visions in American Film Classics*, edited by John R. May—none have really put in systematic form the approach that I hope to elaborate in the following pages.

The approach that I have developed is indebted to two major sources. One stems from my graduate student years at the University of Chicago Divinity School when new students had to study seven different fields of learning and pass comprehensive exams on them. Among the seven were several new "dialogical fields", which were pioneering efforts at relating theological studies to other secular fields in the University. I chose one of those fields—Ethics and Society—for my main work and calling.

But the one of interest to us here was a field called Religion and Art. One of the founding documents of the field was an essay written by a young Quaker professor, Preston Roberts. The essay had appeared in a 1951 issue of the *Journal of Religion* and was entitled "A Christian Theory of Dramatic Tragedy," which was a synopsis of Roberts's doctoral dissertation. In that essay he argued that serious dramas could be interpreted according to three basic kinds of narrative that underlay them.

He identified three narratives—the Christian, the Greek, and the skeptical—and pointed out how each handles character, plot, atmosphere, and tone differently. It was a brilliant essay that opened the eyes of many of us to deeper meanings in western literature. The following pages in many ways comprise a reinterpretation and elaboration of that seminal essay.

The other source for my classes in film interpretation and for this book came from the Ecumenical Institute, a Protestant renewal movement of almost monastic character that flourished in Chicago in the 60s and 70s. The "E.I." was dedicated to renewing Christian faith and life by a highly disciplined and intense pedagogy. Among the courses they developed was their basic introductory course, Religious Studies I. After teaching the basic Christian themes of God, Christ, Spirit, and Church in impressively imaginative and colorful ways, the compressed learning experience ended with viewing a perfectly secular movie through the lenses of the Christian themes developed earlier.

The movie was *Requiem for a Heavyweight*, starring Anthony Quinn. The RS 1 teacher would move through a schedule of questions in a "directed conversation" that illuminated the underlying meaning of the movie. The course argued that at it deepest level *Requiem* expressed the Christian themes of the judgment of God, the grace of Christ, and new life in the Spirit. The theology undergirding the E.I. approach was informed by a radical Christian existentialism that I soon modified, but the pedagogical approach was very useful to me. I found that it was a wonderful vehicle for teaching students the theoretical framework I had learned from Roberts. It lent itself to lively discussion without the confusion that often accompanies such conversation in a classroom. In short, the basic framework of meaning could be applied to a number of different movies in a richly dialogical way.

At the outset of each course I tell the students that the learning curve will be steep and that they will never view films the same way again. Such confident claims have been pleasantly realized not only in the classroom, but also in churches, movie discussions in the home, continuing education events, and other formal assemblies.

I write the book for two purposes: to produce the kind of text for my courses I have always wanted but had to supply in a collection of hand-outs; and to offer my approach to a broader readership that may find it helpful in both formal educational settings and informal gatherings. Both purposes, if fulfilled, will enhance my ultimate aim, which is to help people see the deeper meanings in serious films.

As already mentioned, my approach is indebted to Preston Roberts and to the Ecumenical Institute. Professor Roberts has recently died, and the Ecumenical Institute is no more. But their creative contributions will live on in this work, which is a token of my gratitude to both. The book is an attempt to be both intellectually enriching in its theoretical proposals and practically useful in its offering of pedagogical aids. The appendices include not only a list of suggested movies that are amenable to the approach developed here, but also a schedule of questions that can be moved through in a guided discussion of the meaning of a film.

There are serious methodological questions involved with any approach to film interpretation. These questions concerning the theory of interpretation are similar to those in the fields of literature and drama. Indeed, many books are devoted to theories of interpretation. I will not delve into such theoretical concerns in any depth, but shall rely on a much more pragmatic approach. The proof will be in the pudding. Lengthy reflections on methodology must await another time, or, most likely, another author. If my approach is effective in illuminating the deeper levels of meaning of serious movies without violating their basic integrity, I will rest my case. I suspect most readers will be satisfied with such a strategy.

I wish to thank all the persons who have encouraged me to put this into print after positive encounters with my approach. I also wish to thank Roanoke College, whose sabbatical program has allowed me the necessary time to put these long-collected thoughts into a book, and to Karen Harris, who expertly fashioned a rough manuscript into a camera-ready text.

Robert Benne
Roanoke College

Chapter 1

THE IMPORTANCE OF MOVIES

A visit to a video shop any where in the world is a mixed experience. On the one hand, I am awed by the number of films stocked, the people shopping, and the rentals made. When I walk up and down the many aisles of titles, however, I am more than a little depressed. Ninety percent of the films are junk; most appeal to the human thirst for sex and violence or other sorts of cheap thrills. What's more, they are of low quality. The acting is bad, the scripts are unbelievable, and the message is usually shabby at best. On the other hand, one can rent, purchase, or order the best films that have ever been made. Parents can purchase movies that are supportive of the values they want to teach their children. Adults can procure high quality movies that deal with the most profound issues of human life. Or they can acquire films of unsurpassed entertainment or educational value.

Billions of videos have been rented and bought in the decade of the 90's, far more than the number of books lent or sold. Students in the typical college classroom have seen far more movie videos than they have read books. There is no contest. It seems that, for better or worse, films are becoming the modern person's literature of choice. The film narrative is replacing the written.

As John May puts it:

> The video-cassette revolution makes it possible at the beginning of the 1990s
> for us to rent film classics from our local video outlet just as our ancestors
> for generations, indeed centuries, have taken books home from the bookstore
> or library. At the risk of becoming overly apocalyptic, I wonder if video
> tapes will not shortly become the principal texts that our children and
> grandchildren take home.[1]

Certainly there is a dark side to all this. The vast majority of movies for
rent in the video shop or offered on TV are appallingly banal. It is hard to
know whether the tastes of the masses stimulate producers to make such
awful stuff or whether the producers actually lower the tastes of the
masses by giving them such tripe over the long run. There is no doubt a
case for both ways of looking at it. Fortunately, the future of both the
video and television industries will be marked by the proliferation of
choice, which will enable the discerning buyer to select high quality
films. But such a proliferation of choice doesn't do much for the elevation
of popular taste where the very capacities for discerning choice seem
lacking from the beginning.

If the substance or content of films is suspect, such is also true of the
medium of film itself. On the one hand, the immediacy and ease of access
of movies seem to make film-watching a passive and lazy affair. One
allows the cinematic experience to wash over oneself. This seems a far
cry from the demands that a good book makes upon a reader. One must
read, imagine, understand, and make many connections for oneself, in
one's mind. It seems that movies do all that for you and thereby weaken
the active capacities of the mind. Who wants their child to abandon
reading for hours of video or TV watching?

But this ease and immediacy should not lure us into thinking that
films do not affect persons deeply. True enough, people can superficially
engage a movie just as they can a book. It can roll by one without making
much of an impression. However, even such weak encounters may have a
more profound effect than first thought. Robert Heffner, an historian,
quotes Oliver Stone's observation about his own movie, *JFK*: "It's one of
the fastest movies...It's like splinters to the brain. We have 2,500 cuts in
there, I would imagine. We had 2,000 camera set-ups. We're assaulting
the senses...in sort of new-wave technique. We want to get to the
subconscious...and certainly seduce the viewer into a new perception of
what occurred in Texas that day."[2]

Rudolf Arnheim contends that seeing a good movie is a powerful encounter with a subject matter, that "visual perception...is not a passive recording of stimulus material but an active concern of the mind."[3] What unfolds in motion on the screen catches us up into its world before we are able to reflect on it. We are often absorbed whether we want to be or not. As we move toward a future of ever more sophisticated visual communication systems, such as through the technology of "virtual reality", we are likely even more to be caught up in the reality that the film itself offers. The Pied Pipers of video will become the definers of reality for more and more people, particularly the young, who are already accustomed to and enamored of this medium.

With all this in mind, it becomes highly important that we teach people to become discriminating viewers of film. We spend years teaching our young to read a book properly, but scarcely any time on teaching them to select good films and to view them with intelligence. As the *London Times* put it:

> Education about film is not rising at a fast enough pace, however. Film has a power on the popular imagination of the world like that of the novel a hundred years ago. Within days of Dickens's works being serialized in Victorian London, they were being reprinted, without permission, in New York. Now a Hollywood movie will be watched in Paris or Tokyo within weeks of its American premier whereas a novel, even by our most celebrated authors, will take years now to be translated and published abroad.[4]

The Times went on to suggest that viewers need to become more literate about films. By that, the editors meant that viewers should know more about the "techniques of film-making." Without disagreeing wholly with that suggestion, I would argue that viewers need more help on two other fronts. The first has to do with developing the ability to choose films of quality. This would of course include training in the techniques of film-making. The second task is, to my mind at least, as important as teaching persons about the methods of film as a medium. It has to do with **understanding** those quality films at their depth. Just as great works of literature can be read superficially, so can great movies be viewed in ways that miss the meanings they convey.

So, in this era when the primary story-tellers will use film rather than paper to convey their narratives, it is very important that we press forward with the education of the viewer. The following represents such an effort.

Chapter 2

MOVIES AND MEANING

A Variety of Approaches

Why all this fuss about the meaning of movies? Many of my acquaintances do not welcome my critical comments about a movie after we have viewed one together. (I've learned not to belabor the point with those who don't want to be bothered.) Such reflection seems to destroy the simple entertainment value of the film. These friends want to go to the theater to be entertained and diverted, not to be pressed into questions about the meaning of life. Certainly many movies are made mostly for entertainment and aren't very amenable to deeper levels of analysis. Many thrillers, mysteries, comedies, and adventures are meant to be pleasant (or unpleasant!) diversions and probably ought to be taken that way. Let's not burden them with roles that were not intended to play.

Indeed, most film reviewing done in newspapers and magazines approaches **all** movies according to their entertainment value. The reviewers comment on the believability of the characters and plot, the excitement generated, the quality of the camera work, the beauty of the scenery, and the performance of the actors. They advise you to go or not to go on the basis of the entertainment value they perceive in the film. Under this approach, movies that are not "exciting" or "entertaining" are neither seen nor reviewed. Further, high quality movies with deeper "messages" are never given their due as conveyers of meaning about human life and destiny. Movie-goers are on their own with regard to such deeper meanings.

While we must for the most part respect people's own interpretation of their intentions in going to movies, there is some room to doubt that entertainment is the only thing going on. In Chapter 1 I already mentioned that film as a medium may have more of an effect on our whole being than we think. Let's deepen that observation by hearing what T. S. Eliot thought about the effect of any work of the imagination on us:

> If we, as readers, keep our religious and moral convictions in one compartment, and take our reading merely for entertainment, or on a higher plane, for aesthetic pleasure, I would point out that the author, whatever his conscious intentions in writing, in practice recognizes no such distinctions. The author of a work of imagination is trying to affect us wholly, as human beings, whether he knows it or not; we are affected by it, as human beings, whether we intend it or not.[5]

A serious, well-made film may impart more to us than we bargain for in our quest for entertainment. A "higher" approach to film, suggested by Eliot above, is offered by more "high brow" reviewers, whose status we generally recognize by calling them "film critics." They operate at what Eliot called the aesthetic level. They have a keen eye for film-making as a craft. That includes the excellence by which a narrative is constructed— the credibility of its characters, the dramatic tension of its plot, the ambiance of its atmosphere and the intentions of its creator. The critics further reflect on the capability of the actors, the technical quality of the camerawork, direction, sets, special-effects and music. They may even get into how the unique characteristics of film as a medium are marshaled successfully or unsuccessfully. Or they may place the film under review in the context of a whole series of films produced and/or directed by the same person.

Such an approach certainly enables the viewer to make discriminating judgments about which films she wants to see. It also helps a viewer assess the quality of the film she views. Moreover, the best critics—such as a Stanley Kaufmann of *The New Republic* or a Pauline Kael of *The New Yorker*—transcend this aesthetic approach to film. Operating from visions of life which they never make explicit, they comment on the meaning of the movie. Drawing generally on a chastened humanism, they point to the insights into the human condition imparted by the movie under review. They examine themes and issues explored in the film. As humanists of a secular bent, they rarely comment on the religious meaning of a film, or, when they do, it is in a very hesitant way. (One exception to this general observation is the critic Michael Medved, who reviews movies for a television program, lectures, and writes critically about Hollywood's aversion to portraying religion honestly, if at all.)[6]

Moreover, they scarcely ever hazard a more systematic interpretation of the whole movie. This is an age of hesitancy; the more savvy reviewers are reluctant to offer interpretations based on their own philosophies of life even if they have such.

Other critics, however, are not so reluctant to interpret films systematically according to a particular vision of life. These critics generally write for journals or magazines of a more ideological bent. They may be Marxists who interpret films through the prism of class analysis. They may operate out of specific school of psychology in clarifying films, offering Freudian or Jungian insights into their meaning. They may view films for their social or political importance, interpreting them according to their strongly held convictions. Increasing numbers of critics view films through feminist lenses, detecting with sharp eyes the evidences of sexual exploitation, oppression or, more happily, liberation.

All of these approaches are potentially useful to the inquiring viewer, though in specific instances they may be wooden and unduly ideological, forcing movies into categories that don't become them.

Each may offer an insight into a film with many layers and dimensions of meaning. But they don't exactly get at what I think is most helpful—the underlying meaning of the whole narrative as it unfolds before us on the screen. They don't elaborate a coherent and systematic interpretation of the deepest and most expansive significance of the movie. It is to such an approach to movie interpretation that we now turn.

The Approach of This Book

Our approach to the interpretation of film is based on the assumption that serious narratives—whether in film, drama or literature—express a vision of life. A film director who aims at portraying a serious drama at the same time conveys a perspective on the meaning of human life. A movie-goer who attentively engages a serious film receives an interpretation of the way life is. In other words, seeing is believing, or better put, seeing is receiving someone else's believing and then deciding whether or not to accept that believing for oneself. I will argue that such is **generally** the case with serious movies.

That said, it is important to note that there are significant and profound movies that do not express a vision of life. They probe more discrete issues and themes. Thus, I do not claim that my interpretative apparatus is able to account adequately for all serious movies. No doubt other categories of interpretation must be elaborated to cover those that seem enigmatic to me, or that escape this sort of narrative analysis altogether.

Elements of Vision—Elements of Narrative

What we have called a view or vision of life is made up of several important elements. A vision expresses a belief about the nature of the processes of life that we are caught up in as we live our lives. Are these processes benevolent, liberating, oppressive, death-dealing or perhaps neutral, maybe even absurd? Is life out to get us or is it out to bless us, or something in between? These processes of life include our day-to-day struggles, our encounters with persons, and events that make up our personal histories. They have a beginning, middle, and ending in the story shown on the screen before us, just as they do in our own lives.

But these processes are colored by a second important element in any profound vision of life. The author or film-maker expresses convictions about the ultimate environment in which the characters' lives, and by extension, our own, are played out. These convictions about the ultimate reality that envelopes and impinges upon our personal stories are sometimes implicit and indirect but at other times are very explicit and direct. All are wagers about the nature of our lives and the nature of the final reality within which our lives take place. They are responses to basic questions about the grand context of all particular human stories. What are the basic conditions under which human life must be lived, its limits and possibilities? Are these background conditions, as they impinge upon and shape particular human stories, supportive or hostile to human aspirations? What do such background conditions suggest about the value, origin, and destiny of particular human lives?

A third element in such a vision is its estimate concerning the nature of human nature. In more old-fashioned language, there is an estimate of the nature of "man," meant generically. A serious film has an implicit or explicit assessment of human character. It aims at answering deep questions about the nature of the human. Are humans basically noble? Caught up in an internal bondage? Perverse and hopeless? Irrepressibly and ultimately successful in overcoming their challenges? Further, this perspective on human nature deals with other questions. What happens when this particular human meets the challenges provided by life? Where does a person start at the beginning of the story, what happens to her in the middle, and where does she end up at the finish? What kind of human values are exemplified in the character, as she undergoes the changes and chances of life? What sort of way of life is directly or indirectly commended by the human action before us?

A fourth element in a vision has to do with the presenter's own attitude or posture toward the story he has told. Does he have affection toward the material just presented? Does he stand ironically at a distance, wryly skeptical of what is going on? Does he have disgust for both the characters and their fate? In other words, a vision presented always has the clear or perhaps faint mark of the presenter.

These elements of the vision that I claim is conveyed in serious movies are at the same time elements of narrative. This is not simply coincidence, because the theory of interpretation I am employing follows those theorists who believe that the elements of narrative constitute a vision. Indeed, what I have called the elements of a vision are termed by these theorists "elements of narrative."[7] They designate these elements of narrative: plot, atmosphere, character and tone. These correspond to the elements of vision which I elaborated above. Taken together, these elements of narrative constitute a intelligible vision of life. Each element fits with the other in a coherent way to project a compelling vision. Great works of dramatic art then, it is argued by these theorists, communicate deeply-held convictions about the nature of human existence.

So, for example, what we will later develop as the Christian Story— or Christian Narrative—has a particular way of handling plot, atmosphere, character, and tone. The Greek Story has a discernibly different way of combining these elements into a distinctive vision. Thus, an author or film-maker, will generally produce a narrative that is recognizable as a Christian, Greek, American, or skeptical story. We will be able to identify these stories by pointing to the way each handles the elements of narrative.

There are several issues we must deal with here before we move on. The first concerns the plurality of stories. How can stories of so much variety fit into these basic types? Of course there is a sense in which no two stories are alike. There **are** different characters, twists of plot, atmospheres, and tones, according to each unique film. There are also stories that obviously are not amenable to our approach. They may simply be constructed to amuse or thrill. Or their stories may escape any of the basic types of narrative we have suggested. Or they may have no coherent narrative structure at all. But it is our contention that most thoughtful movies in fact do have profound meanings about life that are conveyed by their underlying narrative. It is the challenge of interpretation to discern them. To quote Wesley Kort:

> Recent narrative theory has been engaged in just such a task. Diversity is viewed as a surface matter. At one level, everyone has a story and everyone's story is unique; but at a deeper level, constants appear. These constants, often grouped under such headings as functions and actants, constitute a complex but finite set or system of possibilities. The term narrative, when used in the singular, refers not to surfaces but to a deep structure which can anticipate the many variables in the plural.[8]

In other words, meanings are encoded into serious movies at a deep level that our approach aims at decoding. At that level the elements are constructed into a coherent whole that convey a vision of life. The deeper narrative structure may or may not be intended by the creator of the film; but it is there and can be discerned by the educated eye. It is the intent of the following pages to impart the approach that will make such discernment possible.

Several questions follow. One has already been discussed, but others are also important. Does the creator of the film have to have a conscious intent to convey such a set of meanings? By no means. A fine writer, director, or producer will construct a credible story that grasps the imagination of the viewer. The encoding may go on without conscious intent. However, many thoughtful creators do in fact have in mind the full meaning of what they convey. But it is finally irrelevant to our analysis whether or not the creator intends such an expression of meaning.

It is important to note, though, that the attitude or posture of the creator to the narrative she has created does make a difference. The creator can distance herself from the story with irony or humor, or she may have contempt for the underlying narrative. Or she may vigorously affirm it with a positive affection for it. The tone—the attitude or posture of the creator—will then make a difference as to how the narrative is received into the imagination of the viewer.

Does this approach represent, on the other hand, a crude imposition of meaning on the film by the analytic framework itself? That is, does this approach entail violence to the integrity of the film? Is the meaning simply in the eye of the beholder? Again, the answer to these questions, I believe, is no. On the contrary, it is our contention that our approach actually points to objective elements in the movie itself. Serious movies **do** construct a character in a particular way, identifying the character's main challenge or predicament in a specific way. Plots in fact do move in certain directions in each of the basic narratives—deep structures—that we have identified. The Christian story combines character, plot, atmosphere, and tone in an objectively identifiable way, as do the Greek, American, and skeptical stories. The underlying narrative conveys a vision of life. The viewer does not simply impose this vision on the film.[9]

Where do these narratives—these deep structures—come from? Are they unconscious or subconscious archetypes in the mind of the creator of the film or novel that bubble up in and through the creative process? Are they transpersonal and transcultural structures in our souls, as a Joseph Campbell, among other Jungians, might argue? Or are they unique creations of each artist, drawn out *de novo* by the ingenuity of his imagination.

It seems that neither of the above interpretations is adequate. Rather, it seems more likely that these narratives are carried by deep-running cultural traditions that shape and form the hearts and minds of their participants. Basic narratives are the main way that a culture transmits its meaning and value system. The narratives are the culture's myths—in the sense of paradigmatic stories—that communicate its vision of human life and destiny. As myths of this profound sort, they help people interpret what is happening to them and their compatriots, they relate persons that receive them to larger realities beyond themselves, and they provide a model for the way they should act.

Religious movements are often at the root of these cultural myths. Christianity, for example, has a specific vision about what the human predicament is, how it is faced and remedied, and what life on earth ought to be like. This vision is recorded in the biblical narratives that have so powerfully conditioned life in the Western world. Believing Christians further affirm that these biblical narratives are trustworthy witnesses to events that happened in history, events that are the revelation of God. In those revelations the truth about ultimate reality, the world, and human life and destiny has been decisively clarified. Thus they look upon the biblical narrative as the vehicle of sacred truth.

Because the West has possessed millions of Christian believers over thousands of years, it is inevitable that the Christian vision—borne by biblical narrative—has profoundly penetrated the culture of the West. Even those moderns who have long departed from explicit Christian belief and allegiance are yet heavily influenced by the Christian vision of life. If they are artists they are likely to have many vestiges of this vision deep inside their psyches. These themes will then appear in their work, sometimes detached from their explicit religious roots, but nevertheless present in dramatic form. Others who yet have a living connection to the Christian vision may explicitly connect these deeply running human themes with their religious roots. In the following exposition of the Christian story as it appears in movies, we will discern both implicit and explicit examples.

The Christian vision is obviously not the only vision of life that shapes the world, or even Western culture. Indeed, one of the major characteristics of modern life is the imaginative portrayal of many visions of life. The modern person is required to choose among them, be they skeptical, American, or Greek, all of which are powerfully expressed in contemporary movies.

The Greek story, of course, comes from antiquity. It is present in Greek philosophy and drama but has its roots in Greek religion. The Greek vision has had an immense effect on western life. Often it has been in combination with the Christian vision, but this alliance, while creative, has also been an uneasy one. The Greek vision continues to be powerfully present in artistic works, including films.

The American story—the American Dream—also has religious, or at least quasi-religious, roots. Biblical themes have been adapted to the American scene to produce a particularly powerful myth about the promise of human life. This myth has been repeatedly ensconced in American movies. It has functioned to enable Americans to give an interpretation of what is going on in their lives, to what larger realities they are related, and of what patterns of behavior they ought emulate.

The skeptical story is not religious in origin. In fact, it would be more accurate to say that it emerges out of the loss of religious belief. But it is pervasively present in modern western culture. It appears in movies in a more self-conscious and explicit way than the other two stories, partly because it is of more recent origin and therefore more freshly present in the minds of creators of movies. But it also taps currents of conviction historically and contemporarily present in many human cultures, but particularly those of the western world.

So we have many fundamental narratives present in the modern world. They are expressed in modern movies through the deep structures that operate below the surface of the plurality of stories. They make their often subliminal pitch to the viewer as he sits bathed in the sight and sound of vivid experience. It seems important to identify, understand, and critically reflect on these powerful instruments of human meaning. If seeing really is believing, let us perform those activities with as much perception as we can muster.

Chapter 3

The Christian Story

The Biblical Narrative

The biblical narrative—the foundation of the Christian story—includes both the Old and New Testaments, the Hebrew and Christian scriptures. The grand story begins with the creation of all that is from nothing by a loving God. God creates the heavens and earth, and all the creatures therein. As the crown of creation, God creates humankind—male and female—in his image. They are given dominion over the earth and have the capacity for covenantal relations with God and with each other. They are given an Eden in which to live. But, alas, they are tempted by a renegade from God's angelic host. They fall for the temptation and shatter their relationship with God and each other, as well as the earthly Eden they have been given. By their own rebellious and willful action they separate themselves from God. Murder, strife, and misery follow their rebellion.

But God does not leave his beloved creation to stew forever in its own alienation. In due time God calls Abraham to follow his beckoning, promising for Abraham's faithfulness a land flowing with milk and honey, a legacy of many descendants and the possibility of becoming a blessing to all nations. The stories of the adventures and travails of the

patriarchs continue until Israel is taken in bondage in Egypt. Through
Moses God promises liberation from their oppressors. They follow
Moses' directions—which were given to him by God—and they indeed
are freed. Upon liberation, they are offered a covenant by this God who
redeemed them. They are to be his people and he is to be their God. He
gives them commandments to order their lives with him and each other.
If they are faithful and obedient to the covenant they shall experience
shalom (peace) and will be given the long-promised land, many sons, and
the possibility to become a beacon to the nations. They are to be God's
instrument for returning the lost creation to him.

They do not keep the covenant. They fall for idols, they are
disobedient and thereby frustrate God's intentions for them. In doing so
they fracture their own lives with injustice. So God sends prophets to
hold up a mirror to the people of Israel. They denounce the people's
disobedience and call for repentance. Their repeated negative verdicts
lead to the chilling prophetic question: In light of Israel's continued
disobedience, can there be anything more than God's judgment in
history? But when all seems lost, the prophets convey God's continuing
faithful love by setting forth the promise of a new rescue mission. In the
fullness of time, God will do a new thing to retrieve his lost and
disobedient creation.

Christians believe that that new thing—the promised rescue—came in
Jesus the Christ. In his preaching, Jesus announces the in-breaking of the
kingdom of God. He shows signs of the kingdom by his teaching, his
ministry of healing, and by his stunning power over nature. He calls for
repentance for those wishing to enter the kingdom, and pronounces
forgiveness for those who repent. He preaches the radical and extravagant
love of God for all repentant sinners. In pressing forth his message, he
offends the religious authorities of the day, not only by his radical notions
of sin, obedience and grace, but particularly by the claim that he is the
one sent by God to fulfill the promise of rescue. By forgiving sins he in
fact takes on God's role. The authorities combine with the Roman
occupiers to put Jesus to death. A good and innocent man dies a horrible
death on a cross.

All seems to have come to naught. The disciples who have followed
him now abandon him in fear and scatter. But then, so the story goes, a
number of women who loved him find his tomb empty when they go to
visit it. He appears repeatedly in resurrected bodily form to his astounded
followers. They believe that God has vindicated Jesus' claims by raising

him from the dead on the third day. From a dispirited and defeated band of losers, a powerful new movement is born.

Shortly thereafter, when they are gathered to worship and proclaim this Jesus as God's Messiah, a powerful spirit comes upon them that empowers them to do great things. The Holy Spirit renews their faith in God, in Jesus as the Christ, and in their newly found mission in the world to proclaim the wondrous things they have witnessed. This Spirit also enable them to love with the same kind of extravagant love that they believe God has shown them in Christ. Finally, the Spirit stirs hope in their souls, hope that their mission in the world will be fruitful, hope that the kingdom which had already begun in Jesus will be consummated soon, and hope that they might participant fully in the eternal life of God in the new covenant that has been forged for them by God's action in Christ.

The Christian community—the church—had begun. Through preaching, teaching, worship, and particularly in the Lord's Supper—the Eucharist—they are nurtured in the Christian life. They begin reflecting on the meaning of the events they and their forbears in the faith have witnessed. They begin to see that the ignominious death by Jesus on the cross was paradoxically the saving action of God in which he through Jesus took into himself the wrath for the sins of the world. Through sacrificial love God had rescued his people and offered a new covenant to them. Jesus' resurrection is the powerful confirmation that this is so. They need only to accept this offering of love to them with repentant heart and they will be saved and enter into a new life in the Spirit, a life begun now but to be extended into eternal life with God.

That in essence is the Christian narrative. I have sketched it out in bare bones, leaving out the colorful names and stories that flesh it out. But the grand themes are there—the drama of creation, fall, judgment, grace, and new life. The human encounter with the Triune God is laid out in this great narrative. A vision first embraced by only few spreads like wildfire in the dying Roman Empire. The Christian faith became the religion of the realm and over the course of centuries penetrated the whole Western world and much of the Eastern. Its vision of life shaped the deepest aspirations of the West. Even in a later era when Christian faith has waned as the animating spirit of Western culture, it continues to condition deeply the way people perceive life's essential meaning.

The Human Reflection in Life and Film

Christians look at the biblical narrative as the most promising clue about what is happening in their own lives. The biblical narrative enables them to discern the pattern of meaning in their personal history, to relate that history to something much greater and deeper than themselves (the action of God), and to discover a trustworthy model for the obedient life. From the Christian point of view, the Christian story points to the depth meaning of what is going on in every person's life. That is, each person is encountering a particular God in a particular kind of way that has been revealed in the biblical epic. What happened in that macrocosmic biblical drama is happening in the microcosmic drama of the Christian's own life. His life is caught up in a meaningful story.

The great task of Christian self-understanding is to discern the depth meaning of his own life. Drawing upon the many resources of his religious tradition—prayer, devotion, hymns, listening to the Word and studying it, spiritual conversation, reflection—the Christian tries to interpret his own life in the light of the Christian story. This is a challenging task for a number of reasons. God's mysterious action upon us is just that—mysterious. We simply cannot read the ineffable God's action upon us like we read a book. We are caught up in processes that we certainly do not fully understand. Our lives are messy—disturbed by unforeseen events and persons. They are often jagged, discontinuous, perhaps even traumatic or tragic.

On the other hand, they are full of routine continuities that extend from week to week, year to year. Lives are often long. We generally cannot see patterns of meaning until long after events occurred. Powerful happenings create enough turmoil in our lives that we are confused about the present meaning of events. Discernment may come more clearly in retrospect. Furthermore, we do not know the end of our story. We don't even know when we are in the middle since we lack knowledge about the end.

Nevertheless, the challenge of interpretation must be answered if we are to have meaningful lives. The Christian story, or some other powerful story, provides the instrument for such interpretation of our lives, but also for interpretation of serious films. If films convey such meaning, as we have argued they do, they must also be interpreted.

The task of both conveying meaning in films and interpreting that meaning has certain distinct advantages over interpreting our lives. Film or fictional narratives, in contrast to an utterly realistic portrayal of real life, can more directly express the convictions of the author. As Kort says:

> In fictional narrative, events and characters can be subjected to beliefs, for example, while in historical narrative, beliefs must submit to the characters and events. This...can reveal something about ourselves or our world which usually is hidden or has been sensed only faintly before. Fictional narrative has more freedom to turn attention to belief, and its semantic direction leads to realities or possibilities which lie below the surface or on the horizons of our worlds.[10]

Thus, films are compressed distillations of the creator's convictions about life, whether or not those convictions are conscious. The creator expresses them in the elements of narrative. He expresses them in how he portrays: the processes in which humans are caught up (plot), the larger context in which those processes take place (atmosphere), the kind of creatures human beings are (character), the attitude he himself has toward the story he tells.

The interpreter of the film discerns these convictions by analyzing the underlying narrative (deep structure) objectively present in the movie. If it is a Christian movie, its narrative will reflect implicitly or explicitly the great biblical narrative sketched above. If it is Greek, or American, or skeptical, it will reflect the shape of those narratives. Its deeper meaning can be interpreted.

Interpreting films is an exercise that enables us to discern the meaning of the story unfolding before us but it also has existential significance for interpreting our own lives. As we comprehend the meaning of the film we ask ourselves: is my life that way? Is that at depth what is happening to me? Is that what I am up against? Is that the way my life should be lived?

As we answer these questions for ourselves, we are caught up in a complex process. The creator of the movie has, either intentionally or unintentionally, encoded the film with meanings that have been imprinted deeply into the Western soul by the biblical narrative (if it is a Christian film). The viewer can catch the meaning of the film by analyzing the nature of the narrative that underlies it. And then the viewer can relate the meaning of the film, thus interpreted, to his own life. Such interpretations can illuminate portions of his own life that had remained opaque or confused, or they may confirm beliefs that he already had about life, or they may challenge a deep-running set of convictions he carries.

Moments in the Christian Story

The Christian story in both life and film, following the biblical narrative, has three basic moments: the confrontation with God as creator, sustainer and judge; the encounter with God in Christ as mercy and grace; and the meeting with God the Spirit in the gift of new life. A closer look at each moment will be helpful in clearly grasping the Christian story as it unfolds in films.

At the beginning of a Christian story, the character is portrayed as internally bound but externally free. The character can be enslaved to himself or an illusion about himself, an external person, goal or thing or some entity or event that has captured his soul. But the condition of bondage is freely self-imposed, it cannot be blamed on external conditions or events. Further, the character's predicament is an estranged condition which precedes specific acts. The person's enslaved condition has caused serious problems for the person himself, his relations to others, and to his capacity to act effectively in the world.

Nevertheless, the person is supported in the midst of this alienated existence by friends, and by his own evident possibilities for being a competent and effective person. He is also claimed by his duty to others, though in his enslaved state he is not able to fulfill them.

I call this first moment the state of "safe bondage." It is evident that the character is neither healthy nor effective, but yet has come to terms in a pathetic way with his condition. He does not want his safe bondage to be disturbed. Much like the enslaved children of Israel in Egypt, he prefers at least the predictable fleshpots of bondage to the uncertainty of freedom. After all, moving from safe bondage would mean painful change and the character prefers a degraded security to such change.

Biblically speaking, human characters are fallen creatures. They have denied and rejected their possibilities as humans. No one outside themselves can be blamed, but in this first state they want to blame everything or everyone but themselves. They insist on seeing themselves as victims. But yet they are sustained by God in the midst of life. They retain their damaged possibilities as humans, and they are supported by persons who love them but whose love they cannot return. They continue to have obligations to others but fail to live up to them. Yet God does not destroy them in their self-imposed misery. The story remains open.

But God does not let fallen persons tarry forever in their safe bondage. They are moved by events and persons out of that state. That movement may be initiated by a traumatic event that shakes them to their roots, it may be precipitated by an overwhelming obligation to another person that they simply cannot escape, or it may come from the internal promptings of their own deeper person that cannot be satisfied with the misery of safe bondage. At any rate, the main character in a Christian drama is propelled by the forceful processes of life to confront his bondage. He is not allowed continually to escape consciousness of it.

This brings us to the climax of the first moment of the Christian story. The events and/or persons who have been exerting the pressure on the character turn the screws further. The pressure point becomes a pressure cooker, to mix metaphors. This process may or may not be intended by the persons that surround the main character, or the pressure may be increased by events which no one seems to control. But the overall effect is one of extreme challenge. The character's capacities for resistance or denial are torn down. She is made to face her illusory self-definition, or her self-chosen idol. This is a painful process that entails the stripping bare of layers of protection to get to the core issue, the primary sin. No one likes that, so the scenes toward the end of this first moment are full of tension, anger and sometimes violence. But finally there is a moment of clarity. The reason for the bondage is made clear and the character recognizes that. She accuses herself. She becomes aware that her bondage is the result of her own sin and becomes willing to accept the guilt for that sin.

Theologically viewed, this process is the working of God as judge of sinful human beings. It is the work of God as Law, as the One who puts humans on the potter's wheel, painfully cutting into them so that that in the end they might be won over to God and his purposes. So the actions of judgment by the God of Law are not aimed at the destruction of the person. Rather, it concludes the first moment in God's drama of redemption and precedes the second.

There are differences in the Christian tradition about whether these "hard moments" are the work of God or the Evil One. But all elements of the tradition seem to agree that even the works of the Devil can and will be used by God to work toward his primary aim, the salvation of all creatures.

The second moment in the Christian story is the moment of redemption. Once the sinful character has been brought to repentant clarity about his situation, she is offered grace and mercy. The grace and mercy is the kind of extravagant love offered the world by God in the Christ event. It powerfully forgives and affirms the person in spite of and in the midst of his pressure cooker experience. This is the grace event. As such it is freely offered and comes uncoerced from the depths of our experience. It cannot be manipulated by the main character or even by those who love her. It is sheer gift from beyond herself. The character merely receives the liberating moment with gratitude. She is totally receptive rather than active.

The shape of the grace event corresponds with the deepest plight or central sin of the main character. The grace event addresses the repentant sinner where she really needs it. If the deepest plight is one of guilt for a past deed or idolatry, the moment of grace offers release from the bondage of guilt. If the character's central problem is being hung up as a victim by something that happened to her in the past, she is offered release from the weight of that past. So grace may address the past of the character; this refers to the forgiveness of sins so prominent in the Christian tradition.

Grace may also address the present distorted condition of the person. Grace affirms the person **in spite of** her degraded state. This is the unconditional love that affirms humans in their sinful condition. We need, as Tillich put it, only "to accept the fact that we are accepted." So the grace event may deal primarily with the condition of self-hatred or self-negation as well as the sin of pride or idolatry. It bestows a deep-down worth to the character sunk in despair. This does not excuse or legitimate the distorted character or destructive actions of the person, but it does radically affirm the person herself.

In any case, grace is a liberating gift that frees the character from bondage into an open future. She is born again, delivered from the imprisonment of a stultifying past or of an enclosed and ineffectual self, and is enabled to move forward into life. As Roberts puts it, the Christian tragic hero is enabled by grace to move from being an "effect facing the past" to a "cause facing the future."[11]

If this second moment is the middle of the Christian story, the third moment, new life in the Spirit, is the ending of the story. Following the grace event, the character is empowered toward a new life of faith, love, and hope. Faith in this part of the story means the vigorous embrace of life as it is given, in spite of its imperfections and depredations. It is the re-enchantment of the heart to the world that has been given to the character. Instead of viewing life as a burden or even punishment, the revivified character grasps it with zest and resolve.

Further, renewed faith means that the character newly discerns her role in the situation of her life. She becomes intentional with her life. She uses her gifts and capacities, which have been languishing, in decisive new ways. In other words, she becomes an effective person. It is important to remember that the situation of her life has not changed; she is not "off the hook", so to speak. The challenges facing her may be just as daunting as ever. What has changed, however, is her **relation** to the situation. In one way nothing has changed; in another way, everything has changed.

New life further means the capacity to love. The affirming mercy received in the grace event moves through the character to the ones around her. She is able to get outside herself and take up the obligations to the ones she loves. This love can also be translated into a passionate quest for justice for other human beings. The decision for love and justice can mean sacrificial action on the character's part; her affections have been released outward to others. The sacrificial love exemplified in Jesus is often re-enacted in the life of the Christian tragic hero.

New life in the Spirit is accompanied by hope. The character can move forward into the future with confidence. History is not closed to her efforts. They can make a difference. The world is not bereft of God's actions for the improvement of the human condition and human efforts are significant. This does not mean that automatic success will follow. The sentimental happy ending is not a necessary part of the Christian story. But the hope that the quest for love and justice resonate with the ultimately real makes a powerful difference. Faithful, loving, and just acts are grounded in something deeper than the surface events themselves. Human hope can be anchored in the nature of reality itself.

Thus, we have the three moments of the Christian story. The elements of a Christian narrative—its character development, plot, atmosphere, and tone—cohere into a vision of life. As the viewer sees a Christian story unfold, she experiences judgment of the character, forgiveness, and finally joy as the character moves through sin, judgment, grace, and new life.

The Explicit Christian Story in Film: *Tender Mercies*

I have distinguished the explicit from the implicit Christian story. By explicit I mean that not only are all the elements in the narrative Christian as elaborated above, but they are adorned with specifically Christian symbols, words, concepts, and expressions. The characters are often self-consciously Christian and they interpret the unfolding plot according to Christian notions. The atmosphere allows for judgment, grace, and new life and the director of the movie affirms the meaning displayed. In short, the Christian meaning of the movie not only inheres implicitly but yet objectively in the elements of narrative; it is also explicity attached to the surface of the story itself. The Christian meaning of the story is straightforwardly expressed.

A heartening development in recent years is the appearance of many quality films that are explicitly Christian. *The Mission, Trip to Bountiful, The Fisher King, Places in the Heart, Babette's Feast, Terese, Tender Mercies, Sling Blade,* and *Dead Man Walking* come to mind, though that is certainly not an exhaustive listing.[12] Though I would very much like to elaborate a number of them, economy dictates that I select one. *Tender Mercies* is my choice.

Tender Mercies

This fine movie, directed by Bruce Beresford and starring Robert Duvall, is set in the flat, open spaces of Texas. It is "big-sky" country where country and western music is big time. The film opens with a drunken brawl between two vagabonds in a small, run-down, isolated, motel. They are fighting loudly and profanely over the last dregs of a bottle of bourbon. When morning comes one of the drunks has already fled, letting Mack Sledge (Robert Duval) hold the bag. Embarrassed and hung over, he approaches the young woman owner of the motel to apologize for the mess he and his buddy have left behind and to confess that he has no money to pay for their rent. He offers to work off his debt and she reluctantly agrees, making him promise not to drink while he works.

In the course of the following weeks he stays off the bottle and works well. He comes to know the young son, Sonny, and his mother, Rosa Lee, who turns out to be a young widow struggling alone to make ends meet by running a decrepit gas station and motel. From the beginning it is clear that Rosa Lee is a strong woman of integrity. She is deeply Christian in a matter-of-fact and steady way. She observes traditional Christian practices with regard to sex and marriage and she attends her Baptist church regularly and sings in its choir. Interestingly enough, such a "straight" character is portrayed with great affection and attractiveness. She even gets Mack to church with her and Sonny, where Mack is asked after the service by the preacher whether he has been baptized. He replies that he has not.

While Mack stays on the wagon and is steadied by the developing love of Rosa Lee, he is still uneasy, smoldering with some deep but unexplained discontent. He is also developing a love for Rosa Lee and an affection for Sonny, who constantly wonders about his real Dad who was killed in the Viet Nam War.

So we see Mack in his "safe bondage". He has something within him that creates great unease in his life, but does not really want to face it. He is surrounded by the love of Rosa Lee and the affection of Sonny. But nothing really quite clicks. He seems ever in danger of lapsing back into violent alcoholism. Even though he has asked Rosa Lee to marry him and she has accepted, the viewer gets the feeling that there is a powder keg in Mack, just waiting to go off with great damage to all concerned.

Mack's past begins to be clarified when a reporter from a metropolitan newspaper seeks to interview Mack. We find out that Mack was a famous country and western music writer and singer. But, the reporter suggests, he has lost his capacities through drink and violence. He is divorced from Dixie Scott, a still famous country singer who continues to sing and record Mack's songs. He is barred from seeing his daughter, Sue Ann, who is in Dixie's unsteady custody. Mack refuses to talk to the reporter but does talk with a group of young men who have their own country and western band and have somehow found out that Mack Sledge is virtually in their back yard. They want him to help them but he pretty much cuts them off and goes back into his shell.

However, the plot thickens when Mack finds out that Dixie is performing in a nearby town. We begin to get inklings that Mack would like to return to his former life of stardom, bright lights and the fast track. He listens to Dixie sing his song, whose key line is "I'm still going crazy over you." He tries to see her after the performance and the meeting ends disastrously. They are like fire and ice. She warns him to stay away, especially from his daughter, who is now an indulged young woman close to twenty. On his way out, however, he talks with Dixie's business agent, Harry Silver, and offers Harry a song he has written. He wonders whether he still has the touch.

Upon returning home, there is great tension between Mack and Rosa Lee, whom he has since married. She resents his going to see Dixie. He responds meanly.

A few days later Harry returns the song that Mack had offered. He tells Mack it isn't any good. Mack's apprehensions escalate. However, instead of an explosion, a very touching moment ensues between Mack and Rosa Lee. He cries, "What's wrong with me? Why am I trying to get back into that world; I don't give a God damn about any of it!" Rosa Lee comforts him by telling him she loves him and that every night in her prayers she thanks God for his tender mercies to her, for Mack, and Sonny. In an ironic twist, she, who is really the tender mercy God has given Mack, gives thanks for him, who is at this point a mixed blessing at best.

After trying unsuccessfully to sing one of his songs to Rosa Lee, Mack erupts in anger and drives off angrily in their pick-up. He goes immediately to a liquor store to pick up a bottle. All day long and into the night Rosa Lee and Sonny wait vainly for his return. Finally she goes to bed and prays her regular evening psalm: "Show me thy ways, O Lord, and teach me thy paths; for thou art my salvation." Mack finally returns and tells Rosa Lee of his tortuous struggle. He tells how he finally had tossed away the bottle without drinking. He confesses to Rosa Lee that he is still torn by his desire to return to the world of writing and singing. He is able to sing one of his songs to her, "Baby, you're the only dream I've had that's come true," and they are reconciled.

But Mack has not yet come to terms with his demon. He is still bound by it. The young men with the band return to ask him to sing and write for them, but he resists. He still has a desire to have it all—fame, money, the fast life, perhaps even Dixie and his daughter. The pressure continues to build toward the pressure point. That arrives with the unexpected appearance of his daughter, Sue Ann, now a young woman. She asks him if Dixie's accusations about him are true—had he been abusive to both and finally abandoned them? She asks if he will sing again in the big time. He is evasive. Finally, Sue Ann asks Mack if he remembers the song he used to sing to her when she was a child, something to do with a snow white dove. This is a moment of great tenderness and expectation. Sue Ann has come from the past and is inviting him to re-enter his past life, not only with her but with his prior life of singing and writing.

Surprisingly, Mack says he doesn't remember such a song. That ends Sue Ann's efforts to bring him back into his former life. She leaves and Mack stands quietly and pensively in the darkened living room in which he had his encounter with Sue Ann. After quite a time he begins singing the song he told her he hadn't remembered. He sings "On the Wings of a Dove", which tells of the baptism of Jesus and God's sending his love on the wings of a snow white dove.

These moments, I believe, represent the turning point of the story. The encounter with Sue Ann is the sharpest moment of challenge; God is turning the screws on Mack. He can no longer escape his predicament, nor continue clutching the idol to which he is devoted. God the Law is challenging the false image Mack has of himself, a self-image Mack has clung to all these self-destructive years. The essence of his sin is that he has believed he can have it all—fame, fortune, his artistic self-expression, life in the fast lane, and marriage and family. His is a distinct form of pride. Sue Ann has come to him with the most attractive invitation to return to his illusion. If he is drawn back toward her and that life he is a goner because he simply cannot handle it all without breaking apart. By his white lie to Sue Ann he refuses to be drawn back into such a fate. He recognizes his problem. He turns from it. He repents.

His song of baptismal grace coincides with his reception of God's grace. His tomb, the darkened living room, brightens perceptively with his song. He receives the forgiving and affirming grace of God at that moment. God's love has descended on him on the wings of a dove. For Mack, the key focus of grace is upon his inability to accept himself as a man with serious limitations that prevent him from "having it all." His pride has screwed up his life. Grace enables him to accept himself as a limited and flawed human being. It also enables him to be free from the clutching allure and guilt of his past life. Liberated from the past, he is able to move into a different kind of future with a new-found acceptance of himself. This has all been made possible by a divine grace from beyond himself.

Additional evidence that this is the pivotal moment in the film consists of three signs of new life. The most obvious and dramatic of these signs is his baptism. The Sunday following his encounter with Sue Ann becomes the baptismal day for both Sonny and Mack. Consistent with the Baptist tradition, their baptisms are a symbol of their accepting Christ and beginning a new life. That acceptance and new beginning happened for Mack in his living room a few days earlier.

Further, soon after the turning point Mack again meets Harry Silver, Dixie's business manager. This time Harry approaches Mack with an aggressive offer to buy some songs from him. Harry's earlier refusal had obviously been a put-up job by Dixie. Harry also brings the disturbing news that Sue Ann has eloped with a ne'er-do-well musician. Mack says he knows nothing about Sue Ann's whereabouts and he refuses to sell any songs to Harry. He says he has other plans for any songs he has written or will write.

Finally, as evidence of new life, Mack confesses everything about his earlier life to Rosa Lee, including the fact that he had been married twice before. The tawdriness of the his past comes out and she fully accepts him in spite of all. He is now able to enter the future as the real Mack Sledge, not as the illusion he had projected for himself. Rosa Lee also talks about the hurts of her past. The two are drawn closer together; the former obstacles to their mutual love have been overcome.

Mack now fully enters his new life. He casts his lot with the small-time band of young men who have been pursuing him. He consents to write songs for them. He appears with them at a gig and sings his songs. His final song is the one he had earlier sung to Rosa Lee, "You're The Only Dream I've Had That's Come True." Other relevant lines: "Things started changing with your touch," and "I'll be everything this man can be." The crowd loves it. The two dance elatedly with each other while Sonny remarks to his friends that he really likes his "Daddy", a designation he has not used with regard to Mack before. Mack has down-sized his expectations to the scale that he can handle. He has discovered his real priorities—the love of his wife and son over the appeal of a fast life he cannot manage. This, combined with his intention to work with the young band in their musical efforts, constitutes his true calling.

But new life does not mean easy life. Just as Mack and Rosa Lee are leaving to celebrate their new partnership with the young men in the band, a phone call brings the shocking news of the death of Sue Ann in an automobile crash. Mack returns to Dixie's mansion for the funeral. He grieves without falling to pieces, contrary to Dixie who hysterically shrieks with self-pity. He is not tempted by his former life.

Working in a garden upon his return, Mack anguishes over why this tragic event fell upon his daughter and not himself. He wonders about the "why's" of life: why did Rosa's love envelop him, why is he the recipient of God's tender mercy and Sue Ann lies dead? "I've got no answer to anything.....I guess I just don't trust happiness." Rosa Lee embraces him to still his turmoil.

Calm passes over him—almost in the manner of Job's submission to God—and Sonny returns home from school. Mack gives Sonny a football and sings "On the Wings of a Dove" as they go into the field to toss the ball around. Rosa Lee watches them as the final song plays in the background: "You've gathered up the pieces of my life....the glory of bright lights can't compare with you."

The three moments in the Christian story—bondage and judgment, grace, and new life—are clearly portrayed in this film. Moreover, they are accompanied by explicitly Christian interpretation of both characters and events. The lyrics of the songs alone carry much of the explicit commentary. Further, the atmosphere of the movie makes clear that human life can be redeemed in principle and sometimes in fact. The director warmly affirms his whole project. One couldn't ask for more clarity in a Christian film.

The Implicit Christian Story in Film: *The Verdict*

The meaning of the implicit Christian story is conveyed by the elements of narrative, not by both the elements of narrative and the surface layer of Christian interpretation. The elements of narrative, as we elaborated them in Chapter 2, have to do with the kind of character in the story, the way the plot unfolds, the possibilities allowed by the film's atmosphere, and the attitude of the director toward the material. There need be no "religious tags" on the characters or plots. Indeed, the movie I wish to interpret casts religious functionaries and institutions in a distinctively negative light. Superficially, *The Verdict* is an anti-Catholic movie, but at deeper levels it is both Christian and Catholic.

The Verdict

This Sidney Lumet-directed film stars Paul Newman as a washed-up lawyer. Frank Galvin (Paul Newman) spends most of his waking hours in a Boston saloon, drinking heavily and playing the pinball machine. He has a ramshackle, chaotic office from which he chases ambulances. He watches the obituary page to find out where and when funerals are being held. He shows up at wakes and funerals to solicit the bereaved into making legal charges against those who might be remotely at fault in the death of the loved one. Before he approaches the bereaved, he uses eye drops to clear his eyes and mouth mist to sweeten his breath. More often than not, his prospective clients react in horror and then anger. They, or most likely the funeral directors, throw Galvin bodily out of their funeral homes.

Dignified and professional, his life is not. He retreats to the bar where he repeats stale jokes to his Irish cronies, eats junk food, and plays the pinball machine. Soon after the movie begins, his contempt toward himself erupts into a frenzied destruction of his own office. Sitting amid the ruins of his records and equipment in a drunken stupor, he has nearly reached the end of his tether. The darkened office resembles a tomb; out in the hall a crucifix is visible, peering down on the hopeless scene.

This is obviously Frank Galvin's "safe bondage". Something terrible has happened in his life that prevents him from being a decent lawyer. We don't know what that is, but the symptoms of his estrangement from himself, his work, and from others are painfully clear. He is dead in the water. But he has established a pattern that enables him to survive, albeit at a low level. Though full of despair, he doesn't really want to be disturbed. And, as far as the viewer can see, he has no one to blame but himself.

The dramatic action picks up when his old lawyer friend, Mick, asks him whether he has done anything about the case that he, Mick, had given him. The case is a real gift. It involves a young woman who was irreversibly brain-damaged in a routine process of giving birth. Something went wrong in the Catholic hospital to which she was taken and both she and her baby were lost. She lies in a vegetative state in a state hospital. The Archdiocese of Boston wants to avoid any adverse publicity so it is willing to settle out of court with the family of the young woman. It is offering $50,000, no strings attached. Galvin, as the family's attorney, would get one third of that amount, enough to support his "safe bondage" for quite some time. Unfortunately, Galvin has been so caught up in his drinking that he hasn't done a thing on the case. He takes no thought for the morrow.

Mick tells him that this is the last straw. He'll not give Frank any more cases. Further, Frank has made an appointment with the young couple who have taken responsibility for Debra Ann Kay, the young woman who is now in a vegetative state. He has of course forgotten the appointment. The young couple, Kevin and Sally Donahue, are newly married and poor. Sally is the sister of Debra Ann and has devoted tremendous energy and time to caring for her sister. She is exhausted and the couple want to move and make a new beginning somewhere else. They are anticipating that the settlement will enable them to place Debra Ann in a quality, permanent-care institution. They can then be released from the great burden they have been carrying. They expect Galvin simply to get the money for them. When they come to his office he assures them he will do that.

In preparing for the case, Galvin talks to one of the staff doctors, a Dr. Gruber, at St. Catherine's, the Catholic hospital where the horrible accident took place. Gruber tells Galvin to go for a lot more money than $50,000, because "The doctors killed that young woman through criminal malpractice." Galvin, somewhat shaken, goes to the ward where the woman lies shrunken up in a fetal position. He takes pictures of her and then just sits and concentrates on her. The moment turns into an intense period of meditation on the lives that were lost. He experiences a deep common bond with her suffering and her loss. A mystical connection is forged and he is captivated by her cause. For the first time in many years he has been grasped at the depths of his life, depths he had avoided through drinking and trivial pursuits. Theologically speaking, God will not let him tarry in his "safe bondage." By a combination of external events and internal pressures, he begins to move out of the security of his habitual estrangement. But we can see that that movement will not be smooth or easy.

He looks up Gruber again and Gruber assures him of his help in prosecuting the hospital and doctors. Galvin asks him, "Why are you doing this?" Gruber replies, "To do the right thing.....why are you?" Galvin wants to own the same motivation with all his being. He's on the way to a catastrophe that is finally a triumph.

He immediately goes to the Archbishop's office to meet with him about the case. The Archbishop has upped the amount the Archdiocese is willing to pay to avoid a court battle. The offer is now $210,000, a very substantial and tempting sum, both to the young couple and to Galvin. In spite of this, Galvin says, "I came to take your money but I can't do it. If I take your money I'm lost; I'll always just be an ambulance chaser." Galvin tells the Archbishop he is going to take the case to court.

In his search for himself, Galvin has neglected to consult his client about the decision to take the Archdiocese to court. Nor has he consulted Mick. Mick is horrified. He knows Galvin's weaknesses and he points out that the Archdiocesan lawyer is Ed Kincannon, the most powerful and feared lawyer in town. He is so ruthless Mick calls him "The Prince of Darkness." What's more, he has a huge staff to organize his cases. He is the most formidable opponent imaginable. Mick tells Frank to take the money and run, before it is to late.

The young couple is not so measured in their response to Frank's unilateral decision to go to court. Kevin punches Frank out and Sally responds with tearful fear. Galvin has risked their treasure for the sake of some irresponsible quest for personal rejuvenation. Further, an obstetric nurse that had been in the operating room when Debra Ann was brought in and who might have important information, angrily resists any of Galvin's questions. Frank's decision begins to look quixotic and wrong-headed, to say the least.

Meanwhile, he has struck up a relationship with a Laura Fisher, an attractive divorcee he has met in his favorite bar. They move quickly to an amorous level and Frank begins to confide in Laura. He reveals his ineffectual past but resolves to her that he will finally "do something right." She gives him warm support. Even so, he has not dealt with the bondage of his past. He continues to drink and play the pinball machine, both activities symptomatic of his old life. He almost misses his appointment with the trial judge because he has been playing pinball.

The judge angrily demands that Galvin not bring the case to trial. (The judge is obviously partisan to the cause of the Archdiocese and is unduly chummy with Kincannon.) Galvin, in a sweat, still resists, but the viewer has the sinking feeling that the tide has definitely turned against Galvin, and that he has few weapons on his side.

Indeed, what few weapons he has quickly disappear. Gruber fails to show at a meeting with Galvin; he has gone to the Caribbean for a "vacation." The expert in anesthesiology he hopes will testify against the malfeasant doctors turns out not to be an expert. He is a kindly old black doctor at an obscure women's hospital on Long Island. It is not certain he is even accredited as a doctor, let alone an expert. The obstetric nurse whom he had approached earlier rejects him a second time, screaming at him that "all you so-called professionals are alike....you're whores!" His case is crumbling before his eyes. He runs first to Kincannon and then to the judge to get them to reinstate their earlier offer. They look contemptuously at him as if he were some sort of bug, and tell him the trial will go on.

Kincannon, of course, has prepared a formidable defense of the doctors against Galvin and his client. His staff has delved into Galvin's past and found out how pathetic Galvin really is. Their investigation uncovers the source of the deep wound in Galvin. After a stellar beginning to his legal career, Galvin was wrongly charged in a jury-tampering case. In his naiveté, he had been maneuvered into taking the blame for something his law partners had actually done. He had collapsed in defeat. He lost his marriage and career and descended into an ambulance-chasing shadow of his former self.

From a theological point of view, the Lord of history is turning the screws on Galvin, stripping away the layers of defense that have kept him safe in his bondage. Now that he has moved out of the security of his bondage, his flaws and illusions are being identified and challenged. It is a painful process, but a necessary one if he is to be free of the weight of the past and free to move into the future in a new way.

The pressure continues to mount as Frank flees to the hoped-for comfort of Laura's embrace. The two have become deeply involved and Frank looks to her for solace. He laments: "We are going to lose. It's my fault. It's all over." Instead of consolation from Laura, he gets biting anger: "What are you going to do about it, you baby? If you want sympathy you've come to the wrong place. Grow up! If you want to be a failure, do it someplace else. I can't afford to invest in any more failures!" Frank reels before this unexpected barrage. He retreats to a yellow-painted bathroom where he breathlessly implores Laura to stop. He can't take anymore. Her piercing words have reached into his soul and identified his deeply concealed predicament. His defenses are down, and his tightly held crutch has also been kicked away. He wonders whether he can live without it.

What is it that has been identified as the source of his estrangement? It is the image of himself as a victim. (In his closing speech at the trial this analysis is corroborated.) Ever since his friends betrayed him years ago, he has clutched to his heart the image of himself as a victim. He has allowed that image to define him and he has shaped his life around that pathetic self-portrait. He has not wanted to give that definition up for the sake of something bolder. The terrible prospect of stepping away from his victimhood has prevented him from leading a competent life. Laura's attack destroys his protected self-definition. He has retreated to his tomb where he almost dies. He pleads, "Please, no more. I can't take any more."

The next scene is one in which Frank is sitting peacefully by a bed that holds the sleeping Laura. Frank is fully clothed and calmly watching his beloved. He has passed through his dark night of the soul and come out a new person in the morning. While there is no portrayal of this, I hypothesize that after the severe challenge he has been put through by Laura, he has recognized his sin and opened himself to grace. Mercy has been shown and it has affirmed him as a worthy human being in spite of his past. Grace has released him from bondage to his self-definition as a victim. The burden has been taken off and he is free to live toward the future as a healed human being for the first time. He is a new man as the morning dawns.

The new day brings evidence of new life. When the crooked judge inappropriately attacks one of Galvin's witnesses at the trial, Frank shows spunk by objecting firmly. He upbraids Mick when Mick says that the case is over, that they don't have a chance. On the contrary, Frank argues, "This is the case and we're going to win it."

This is obviously hope in things not yet seen, because the case continues to go badly for Frank. His black doctor "expert" is embarrassed by Kincannon as he testifies on the stand. To top it all off, we are ushered by the camera into Kincannon's inner sanctum where he is offering a large check to a person sitting on his sofa. That person is Laura! Kincannon says, "Welcome back" to a Laura who has obviously had a long relationship with him. He pays her for informing him about Galvin's every move. Kincannon leaves no stone unturned in his efforts to win. But Laura has gotten in deeper than she intended. She has fallen in love with Frank and is in deep anguish about her betrayal of him.

Frank, unaware of Laura's real role, grasps at a final straw. He knows there was an admission nurse at the hospital that fateful night who admitted Debra Ann Kay. The nurse, Caitlin Costello, has mysteriously disappeared. Galvin thinks she has important information. He tricks the recalcitrant obstetric nurse into divulging Caitlin's name and location. Frank and Mick stay up all night calling all the entries with Caitlin's new married name in the New York City telephone directory. Finally, Frank hits paydirt. He makes an appointment to see her in New York under false pretenses, because he knows she would refuse to see him if she knew he was going to draw her into a court battle.

He hops a plane to New York and finds Caitlin. There, in an intense conversation he finds out that the doctors had forced her to change data in her admission report. Debra Ann Kay had entered immediately after she had eaten a large meal and should not have been given anesthesia so soon. The hurried doctors took an ill-advised risk with disastrous results. Debra Ann had nearly died by choking on her own vomit during the delivery. Though she did not die, her brain had been deprived of oxygen long enough to destroy it. Her baby did die. The doctors covered up by ordering the admission nurse to alter the admission report, which had accurately recorded the fact that the patient had just eaten. Horrified by this breach of professional ethics, Caitlin had left nursing and fled to New York. She married and was working in a child-care facility.

Frank convinces her to return to Boston to tell her story. She accompanies him in time to appear at the trial. Meanwhile, upon Frank's arrival in Boston, Mick tells Frank about the perfidy of Laura. Mick had found the check from Kincannon in Laura's purse. The effect on Frank is obviously powerful, but he is not dissuaded from his task as a lawyer. He plunges forward.

The trial comes to an intense climax. Kincannon thinks he has the case sewed up. Galvin shocks the defense with his introduction of his new witness, but they are able to throw doubt upon her testimony. After all, it is the word of one disgruntled nurse against the word of two distinguished doctors. It looks like all will be lost until Caitlin produces the original unaltered admission report, which she had kept all these years just to prove her innocence, lest she be charged with malpractice. Even with this new evidence, the Kincannon forces battle mightily and there is still doubt about the outcome of the trial as it comes to its final chapter.

After Kincannon's strong summation, Galvin rises to the task. He is now operating full tilt as the lawyer he was meant to be. He gives a very eloquent summation. It is a commentary both on his own struggles and on the trial. "Most of the time," he says, "we feel lost." "We are confused and do not know what is true or just. There seems to be no justice. We think of ourselves as victims and we become victims. We become weak, doubt ourselves, our beliefs, our institutions, and the law itself. In the midst of that we pray to God to show us what is just and true. In my religious tradition we are told to act as if you have faith and it will be given to you. Have faith, believe in yourselves and in the law. Act for justice."

The jury returns a guilty verdict and a very large sum is given to the Donahues to care for Debra Ann. The plaintiffs celebrate their victory outside the courtroom. Watching them is a distraught Laura who tries to approach Frank. He rejects her. The film ends with a despondent Laura trying repeatedly to phone Frank. He doesn't answer and we are left with doubts about whether he ever will.

Except for the closing speech, there are few allusions to religion in the movie. Those that are included are negative toward the church and its representatives. But the narrative is deeply Christian. The tragic hero, Galvin, moves through the three moments of the Christian story. At the beginning he appears in bondage to sin of his own making. His victimhood is finally his own responsibility, even though an awful thing had happened to him. He moves through a process in which he is challenged to the roots of his being. In the course of his pressure point experience, his defenses are broached and his predicament is clarified. He has chosen victimhood and is guilty for doing so. He recognizes this, turns about, and is offered a grace that affirms and forgives. He is liberated from his victimhood and the weight of the past that has been created out of that self-definition.

Moreover, this film has a detailed account of the new life that flows from the gift of grace. Galvin's faith in himself, in law, and in life itself is renewed. He is enabled to regain his true calling. He becomes a skilled and committed lawyer again. He acts with courage, decisiveness and tenacity. His life takes on intentionality. Further, his love for Debra Ann Kay is translated into a passionate search for a just resolution of her cause. He takes her burden upon himself and presses it forward vigorously. He suffers in the process. He is again hopeful that his actions will have meaning, that they are not ineffectual. Indeed, he regains his hope that justice may out in our judicial system. He regains hope in ordinary persons' capacity to do justice. Faith, love, and hope are renewed possibilities in his life.

The one jarring inconsistency is Frank's seeming unwillingness to forgive Laura at the very end. However, it must be said that a quick and easy forgiveness would be a lapse into sentimentality. Perhaps there will be room for forgiveness later. The film does not tip its hand. But, certainly from a Christian point of view, Frank ought in time to offer forgiveness. There may never be another chance at marital love for them, because the wounds of betrayal were too great, but there ought to be an opening in Frank's soul to forgive. He has received mercy and grace; he needs to reflect that in his own life. But we do not know what he will do.

Concluding Remarks

We have now elaborated the source of the Christian story, the biblical narrative. We have showed how that story is reflected in human life, both as it is lived and as it is depicted in film. We have demonstrated how the Christian story through its narrative elements—character, plot, atmosphere, and tone—expresses objectively a coherent vision of life. We have been able to recognize that vision in both explicit and implicit expressions on the screen. Our interpretation has not been an arbitrary imposition of meaning on an unsuspecting film.

Shortly we shall move on to other stories. Before that, however, there are a few issues to be examined. One of them has to do with what we have called the implicit Christian story as it is enacted in life and film. Such implicitness suggests that salvation is offered persons without regard to their religious convictions, or lack of them. Does God judge us, redeem us, and give us new life without us knowing about it or accepting it? On one level, the answer has to be yes. In the New Testament Jesus heals many persons without their making confessions of faith in him in response. Nevertheless, they are healed. Likewise, it seems consistent to believe that God brings judgment, offers grace, and renews life among persons who have never heard of Jesus and even among those who have heard but not believed. God, according to the biblical tradition, is free to act in judgment and/or with mercy as He wills. God's will is sovereign, not beholden in any simple sense to human response.

At another level, however, implicit involvement in the Christian story in both real life and in film lacks something extremely important. It lacks the self-conscious appropriation of the **meaning** of the experience. The source of judgment, grace, and new life is not named. The experience is not enlightened by Christian interpretation. Those who experience God's grace are still in the dark. They may call the experience luck or claim it as their own accomplishment. In either case the gift as gift is not recognized. Neither do they know from Whom it comes. Also, from a mature Christian point of view, Christians know they are finally not saved by their experience but by their faith in God's promise in Christ. God in Christ is the object of their faith, not their own experience, which may or may not be gifted with dramatic moments of grace. So mature faith, while it might long for a decisive experience of grace, is finally attached to the objective event of Christ, which to Christians mediates the salvation of God.

Another question arises concerning the implicit Christian film. Why must the underlying source of judgment, grace, and new life be identified as God? Why can't the process be seen as a perfectly human affair? Everything "Christian" about character, plot, atmosphere, and tone can remain the same, just eliminate the notion of God as the agent behind the action. The God hypothesis is unnecessary.

This approach constitutes a very important challenge. On the one hand it must be admitted that some films seem to proceed in such a manner. The "Christian" elements in the narrative are nearly all there, but the story exhibits no traces of divine agency. It is simply a humanist play. Woody Allen's *Hannah and Her Sisters* provides such a case in point. The heroine is finally liberated, but her liberation appears as a matter of her own accomplishment.

Others, such as *Ordinary People* and *Terms of Endearment*, which I count as implicitly Christian movies, could be interpreted according to a humanist frame of reference. None of this would be surprising, since the Christian story has been so powerfully present in the culture of the West. Most of the elements of narrative are there according to their Christian imprint, only the religious roots of the narrative structure have been excised. What was once attributed to God is now attributed to humans. The God hypothesis has been dropped out of the narrative, much as it has been eliminated in modern natural science.

My response to this is properly ambiguous. I admit that a number of what I have called "implicitly Christian" films can be interpreted in this humanistic manner, although it must be conceded by the humanists that the narrative structure itself is indebted to the Christian view of life. Nevertheless, I hold that the "implicit" category is legitimate beyond this concession. The assumption of divine agency in the narrative, it seems to me, is dependent on several things: first, divine agency is a warranted assumption when the plot is permeated with a certain mysterious purpose. The characters do not simply determine the plot through conscious or unconscious agency. Rather, the processes of action seem caught up in something beyond human control, and those mysterious processes seem to move in a purposeful direction. One could call the mystery chance, but then the story becomes much less meaningful. Frank Galvin's story in *The Verdict* is part of a mysterious process that leads from estrangement to new life, and the movie does not suggest that that process is simply the result of chance or a concoction of human decision-making. Its atmosphere suggests more than that.

Second, divine presence is warranted when, in the moment of grace, there is a powerful moment of receptivity on the part of the tragic hero. Something is obviously given, not achieved. Such is the case in *The Verdict* as well as in *Ordinary People* and *Terms of Endearment*. The character has not accomplished liberation through sheer force of will. Nor has redemption come because of the intentions of actions of others, though they in fact may attempt to help the hero. Rather, something has been given that allows self-affirmation and then new life, something that neither the hero nor those around him can control.

The assumption of divine agency depends, then, upon the atmosphere of the movie, whether it allows for the mysterious sense of meaning and direction in the story. It depends further on the tone of the movie, the attitude of the director toward the material. If the director affirms the narrative as a meaningful story, he or she at the same time affirms the mysterious intent also.

Finally, it is important to mention that there are a number of films that have all the elements of narrative in place for a Christian story, but that have characters who finally refuse redemption. These are "failed" or "incompleted" Christian stories. A movie such as *Ironweed* provides a good example. The main character, Francis Phalen, played by Jack Nicholson, is brought to the point of repentance and grace but then decisively turns from it. Then, like the skeptical movie, the character moves toward madness and death.

This brings to an end our rather lengthy exposition of the Christian story. The length represents not only the author's interest and belief in the Christian story, but also provides a detailed framework from which the other stories can be elaborated, compared and contrasted. Other expositions can be briefer because of the space we have given to this chapter.

Chapter 4

The American Story

The Biblical Narrative

The American story shares common roots with the Christian story, though the American roots are grounded more extensively in the Old Testament than the New. The connection of the American mythos with Old Testament themes has long been noticed by scholars. R. W. B. Lewis, for example, in *The American Adam*, showed how America and the archetypical American character are portrayed in an important strand of American fiction as somehow having escaped the Fall. At least their situation-in-life precedes the Fall. In such literature there is a pristine and peculiar innocence about America and its characters, particularly in comparison with the corruption of the Old World and its people.

Perry Miller's famous study of the Puritans, *Errand Into the Wilderness*, demonstrated the Puritan intention of bringing God's true covenant to American shores. Like Israel of old, early settlers believed they were leaving the bondage of Egypt, crossing the Red Sea (Atlantic), and inhabiting the Promised Land. If they were true to the call of God and obeyed the commands of God's covenant, they would not only inherit the land and have many sons, they would also become a "beacon to the nations." God's intentions would have a new career in this new land.

Indeed, we could expect *The Kingdom of God in America*, to use the title of H. Richard Niebuhr's classic study of American history. Martin Marty's book, *Righteous Empire*, traces a similar theme in American life. Old Testament motifs have played a powerful role in shaping the consciousness of Americans. It is therefore likely that they should be formative in shaping the American story.[13]

We have already recounted the basic elements of the Old Testament narrative in Chapter 3, so we need not repeat the whole story. But it is important to emphasize that the narrative has, like the Christian story, a time frame that moves from the past through the present into the future. The first chapter in the story includes the Creation, Fall, the calling of the people of Israel, and the tragedy of bondage in Egypt. The second has to do with the liberation of the people from Israel, the gift of the covenant, and the severe testing of the people in the wilderness. The third, having to do with the future, involves the hope for the promised land. If the people are obedient to God and the covenant he has offered them, a glorious future of land and sons will be theirs.

American self-understanding has been much affected by this primal narrative, as we suggested above. America was thought to be "the new Israel," a redeemer nation in which the true church, the true polity and true humanity would be forged. America was God's exceptional project in the new world, just as Israel was in biblical times.

While the Old Testament narrative shapes decisively the deep structure of the American story, it has been revised and indigenized to fit the American context. A story distant in time and space was adapted to American needs. This revision, however, though quite different in content, is similar in form to the original. Moreover, it is a sacred story. It expresses and affirms what is believed to be a true vision of life. This vision holds up as universal and sacred certain values that are both biblical and American. And it functions as all primal narratives: it helps people interpret what has happened and is happening to them; it relates them to something larger than themselves—a people, a history, and finally to God's action; and it provides a model for life.

The American Dream

Philip Hefner and I argued in an earlier book that the American Dream is America's version of the Old Testament narrative.[14] The basic form of the Old Testament story has been kept, but the content of the Dream is an American reinterpretation.

The Structure of the Dream

The American story begins with a wholesome and innocent character coming from an Eden-like context. Usually it is a rural scene that exhibits great American natural beauty. A decent and loving family is most likely in the background. But the situation is confining. Its geographical and social limits inhibit the character from reaching his full potential. While attractive, this starting point is also a kind of bondage. If the character would remain there he would finally lose the promise of his life. The action begins.

The American Dream challenges everyone to:

1. Shake free of the limits of the past.......

Like Abraham of old and Israel in Egypt, the American is exhorted to leave his inherited place for a journey toward the future, a journey that will lift him beyond his forebears. The American cherishes the freedom to do this, and commends such freedom to all.

This drive to move entails a willingness to leave the context that nourished him, so there is an anti-traditional bias to the American Dream. He might take the virtues and identity learned in the past with him, but the American hero definitely leaves the sustaining past behind. He plays fast and loose with the past.

Free from the baggage, inertias, and corruptions of past civilizations, the American can write with a clean mind and heart on a clean slate. Even within the boundaries of the American territory itself, such a stance toward the past was more than a minor note. The most spirited and ambitious cut their ties with the settled, eastern seaboard and plunged westward where a new beginning could be made.

After the frontier was closed, this shaking free from the limits of the past is simply transferred from geographical to social mobility. The past to be escaped need not be spatial; it can also be social. The American Dream promises that all are free for such movement away from the limits of the past.

2. And to engage in a struggling ascent...

Once the American character shakes free from the limits of his past, he is expected to engage in a movement upward. He is to show **initiative**.

The American hero is to be self-starting and inner-directed. The values he has internalized are to serve as a moral compass that guides this struggling ascent. He is to play by the rules in his ascent, though those rules are not simply a reflection of his social environment. Often they are at odds with the moral and spiritual landscape into which he moves, and part of his struggle is to remain true to those inner signals in the face of opposition or temptation. This heeding of "the rules of the game" is a vestige of the Old Testament theme of covenantal existence.

The quintessential American character always meets daunting challenges. His mettle is tested by these challenges, and the virtues that enable him to overcome adversities are strengthened by the trials that confront him. The inner strengths of discipline, courage, self-confidence, endurance, versatility, ingenuity, and a "can-do" spirit come to the fore. Moreover, a capacity to sacrifice present enjoyments for the sake of the future is affirmed. So, in this period of struggling upward and outward from the limits of the past, the American is to show the virtues that enable such an ascent. And they are strengthened by the tests he meets.

There are obvious Old Testament reverberations here. Like Israel in the wilderness, the American is beset by many trials. His character is tested by these wilderness challenges. As he faces them, he is to heed the call of conscience, a inner kind of convenantal consciousness. The challenges he meets are often generated by wicked characters or death-dealing events. There is a struggle between good and evil. The American, like the Israelite, is on a journey toward a future promise.

Besides these similarities, however, there are many differences between the American Dream and the Old Testament story. In the American story, there is little room for the call of God or for the action of the sovereign God. The American generates his own strength and action, and overcomes the challenges by his own resources. The corporate emphasis of the Old Testament covenant idea is made thoroughly individual. Conscience is internally generated, not received from God's revealed Law.

3. Toward an open and gracious future.

The third moment of the American Dream has to do with the future. If the American hero has shaken free from the limits of the past and has engaged in a struggling ascent in the present, then he can look forward to a gracious, open future. The future will embrace his project. This is a natural occurrence, for the land and society is spontaneously open and welcoming. Opportunity is luxuriantly present for those faithful to the Dream. The American hero is optimistic that such a future awaits him.

The content of the Dream remains closely connected to the Old Testament promise. Land and sons figure as prominently in the Dream as they do in the Old Testament. Beyond these, the fulfillment of the promise has to do with success, broadly defined. Each person defines what success is. It can be the achievement of excellence, wealth, honor, love or victory. But each of those is usually accompanied by the inheritance of land and sons.

Old Testament echoes remain in the American Dream, but there are also important changes. The shalom that accompanies living according to the covenant of God is present in the successful dwelling on one's own land with one's own family, but it is certainly diminished in relation to the Old Testament communitarian vision. Generally it is the family that enjoys the blessings of life, not the whole community. Further, God bestows such blessing in the biblical version, not the land itself as in the American story, though the divine blessing often lurks in the background of the American account.

Thus we have the American Dream, an indigenized version of the Old Testament narrative. Its past, present, and future correspond to the linear frames of the biblical story. Its content is affected by Old Testament notions, but is given a distinctively American twist. Though in some measure secularized in the process of indigenization, it is nevertheless a sacred story. It functions to interpret the meaning of American lives and to relate them to the moving stream of American history, and finally to God's intentions for all human life. The values of freedom, initiative, and opportunity are projected onto a universal screen. All humans should be able to enjoy and take advantage of them. Above all, the story becomes a model for the way life should be. And insofar as it has actually worked that way successfully (and it has been corroborated by millions of American lives), it has become deeply embedded in the culture of America. The Dream becomes a story about human life that has universal appeal. As it appears in movies it expresses a compelling vision of life.

The American Story in Film: *The Natural*

There are many examples of the American story in American films. The classic westerns generally exhibit the deep structure I have outlined above. Movies such as *Shane*, *High Noon*, and *Stagecoach* come to mind. The newer westerns done by Clint Eastwood for the most part follow the

American story. Westerns, however, are certainly not the only filmic expressions of the American Dream. Frank Capra movies like *It's a Wonderful Life, Mr. Smith Goes to Washington*, and *It Happened One Night* are further examples. At a more common level, the Sylvester Stallone *Rocky* series depict the American Dream. John Wayne and Jimmy Stewart played in scores of movies reflecting the American story.

The movie I wish to deal with extensively, however, is *The Natural*, a movie directed by and starred in by Robert Redford. The movie itself is quite different from the novel by Bernard Malamud from which it is adapted. The more ambiguous and tragic elements have been diminished for the sake of a genuinely mythic celebration of the American story.[15]

The Natural

The movie begins in an Edenic American rural setting. The rolling hills and lush farms of eastern Nebraska are gorgeously portrayed. An Adamic American family lives there among other similar families. Mom and Dad Hobbs are right out of a Norman Rockwell painting. Their young son, Roy, thrives in this wholesome atmosphere. He plays in the fields and helps with the chores. Their world is one of perfect, dreaming innocence. Roy and his Dad play baseball and it becomes evident that Roy has a real talent for throwing the ball. As he grows and becomes ever better as a pitcher, his father tells Roy that he has great talent, but must now develop it. "You must go as far as you can." He exhorts him to forsake his bucolic rural environment for the city in order to rise as high as his talent and determination will take him.

As Roy develops into a fine baseball player, he also grows in love for his childhood girl companion. Iris, played by Glenn Close, becomes his sweetheart. Their love is surrounded by all the wholesomeness of pristine nature and loving parents. But if Roy is to "go as far as he can" he must leave Nebraska for the big time. Marriage seems out of the question but their young love is consummated shortly before Roy must leave.

The only discordant element in this idyllic scene is the death of Roy's father. He dies of a heart attack in the arms of his young son. Immediately after the father dies, a violent storm hits the area and a lightning bolt strikes a large tree in the center of the farm place. From a huge splinter of the tree's trunk Roy fashions a bat which he calls "Wonderboy." It seems that nature redresses the balance disturbed by Roy's father's death by offering something almost magical, an Excalibur-like piece of wood that becomes a potent bat in the hands of Roy Hobbs.

(We know from this point onward that reality will be a bit elastic; the mythic character of the film demands that fantastic elements accompany crucial events. In this case, nature conspires to give "the natural" the weapon he needs for his struggling ascent.)

So off he goes to Chicago on the train. He is accompanied by an older baseball man who is to see to it that he gets there safely for a try-out with the Cubs. On the train the two meet a famous baseball player, also on the way to Chicago. The baseball player—"The Whammer"—is obviously a surrogate for Babe Ruth. The Whammer is accompanied by his cynical, worldly-wise agent as well as a big-city sports writer. The Whammer's party treats Roy and his overseer with contempt, prompting Roy's handler to challenge the other party to a contest. He bets that Roy can strike out the Whammer.

A contest is arranged during the next train stop, which happens to be at a small town where a carnival is providing entertainment for the townfolk. The movie captures beautifully the aura of a small town fair of an earlier day. It also evokes the nostalgia of old-timey America when it portrays the baseball contest. The train huffs and puffs as it awaits the outcome of the competition between Roy and the Whammer. The atmosphere of a warm midwestern summer evening is palpable. Even the buzzing of flies and gnats is authentic. The American Eden is brought to life on the screen.

As one might guess, Roy strikes out the Whammer. The arrogant bully is down-sized before our eyes. Roy accepts the victory humbly. Watching all this action is a "dark lady," one Harriet Bird. She embodies all that is inimical to the American Dream. While she loves contests of skill, she believes that real beauty would be best served by the fateful and early death of the winner. She has a deranged tragic view of life. Not only does she gain erotic satisfaction from the death of the hero, she is willing to do the killing. She successfully attempts to lure the innocent and naive Roy into her web of death. But she postpones her sting until they are in Chicago.

There Roy is invited to her apartment. She awaits him in the black garments of mourning. She shoots him and then kills herself. Roy is badly wounded. The lurid details are splashed on the front pages of the Chicago papers. We believe Roy's baseball career has come to a crashing end.

Sixteen years elapse. The scene is now New York. The team is the New York Knights. They are doing terribly and their avuncular manager, Pop Fisher, is beside himself. Irritable and impatient, he knows full well that his role on and stake in the team is threatened by this awful season. Shady criminal figures are poised to take over the club if the Knights don't win the pennant. That would mean the end of Pop and the New York Knights.

Roy shows up as a middle-aged rookie whose contract has been purchased by the Knights for all of $500. Pop stares at him in disbelief; this will help the foundering Knights? Roy refuses to answer any questions about his past, fearing that the scandal of long ago might again nix his chances. Out of disgust and distrust, Pop will not play Roy. Roy sits on the bench game after game. The other players no longer care about baseball. They go through the motions; their real lives happen after the game.

Things look hopeless for everyone but the criminals, who lurk behind darkened windows in an enclosed box in center field. They delight in the collapse of the Knights and are making a killing betting against them. One of the criminals is named Gus Spanos; even the name sounds unamerican. The arch criminal of the gang is a corrupt judge who cannot stand to be in full light. He skulks in the dimly lit office in center field. He also seems to have connections with other corrupt authorities. Another of the cabal is a woman that looks distressingly like Harriet Bird. Her name is Memo Paris and she dates the "star" of the Knights, making sure that he will not play well after all-night bouts with her.

Roy finally gets a chance. He is no longer a pitcher but rather a fielder. But above all he is a hitter. Once in the line-up he strokes hit after hit with his Wonderboy. The team picks up and begins to win. They move up in the standings. The city becomes excited about the Knights. Roy becomes a hero. Thousands of city children look up to him. He has begun his ascent to being the best he can be. And that certainly has not come without struggle. He has had to show patience, fortitude, discipline, and determination. He also plays according to a strict ethic; he plays by the rules of the game he very much respects.

One memorable event of mythic proportions occurs at the beginning of the Knights' winning streak. Roy literally "knocks the cover off the ball," a feat that only occurs metaphorically in real life. The ball unwinds after the cover is knocked off and degenerates into a lumpy mass of tangled string in the hands of the center fielder. The crowd—and the movie-goers—go wild.

However, Roy's struggle is not over, nor have the Knights achieved their goal. The sinister figures are disturbed by the success of the Knights. They meet with Roy to try to intimidate him. They tell him that Pop

Fisher is jinxed. Gus peers with an evil eye at Roy and tells him "You're a loser." They suggest that fate will again strike down Roy and his team. This is a strong challenge to Roy's courage and resolve, considering what he has been through on his painful journey to the big leagues.

The mobsters don't want to risk losing their evil venture, so they concoct a further plan. They order Memo Paris to entangle Roy in a dissolute life with her. Memo jettisons her old lover and puts her moves on Roy. He seems defenseless against such a wiley seductress. His life begins to degenerate into drinking, carousing and fornicating. He quits hitting. The Knights begin to languish. Pop is worried and irritated with Roy but nothing seems to be able to stop his descent into perdition. He has violated the rules of a good life and is paying the consequences.

Enter the woman in white. In the midst of an at-bat after he had ignominiously struck out in his prior appearances, Roy's eyes are drawn to a woman standing in the crowd. She is dressed in white and seems to have a halo around her head. (Is she Gwenivere?) He is transfixed for a moment. He seems to draw invigorating power from her presence and proceeds to smash a home run immediately after his "vision" of her.

He arranges to meet her at a soda shop where they have lemonade. Her wholesome influence has made an immediate effect on his habits. Roy goes home with her and finds out that she lives alone with a young son though she is not married. He begins to tell her his life story and she hers. We realize that she is the sweetheart of his youth whom he left when he went off to become a big league player. Roy becomes uneasy and leaves when Iris tells him that her son is about to come home from school. Moreover, she allows, her son badly needs his father.

Roy's burst of heavy hitting raises the Knights' prospects again, and at the same time raises the anxieties of the mob. They need to do something very effective, so they get Memo Paris to poison Roy. She poisons his food at a reception and he winds up deathly ill at a hospital where he undergoes surgery.

Naive almost to the last, Roy finds it hard to connect Memo with such nasty behavior. When she almost shoots him, he finally makes the connection. He looks her in the eye and remarks: "We have met before." Roy sees the same spirit of nemesis in Memo that he glimpsed in Harriet Bird before she tried to kill him. Fate in the form of a temptress again tries to fell the American hero.

Now that the mob has Roy in a weak position they try to clinch their efforts to squelch him. They send "the judge" to tempt Roy with big money and to frighten him with the threat of blackmail (they have photos of the earlier episode with Harriet Bird). This doesn't work and Roy tells the judge to leave. He has finally figured out the array of forces working against him.

His earlier hitting streak has gotten the Knights into contention for the pennant. It's the last crucial game of the season and Roy is in a hospital bed. He summons his resolve, leaves the hospital and arrives at the park at the climactic moment. He is sent to bat with the winning runs on base. He faces a young pitcher from Nebraska (the Roy Hobbs of long ago returning?) who whistles two strikes by him. He breaks his beloved bat Wonderboy on a foul ball. He no longer has Excalibur. To complicate matters further, the wound from his surgery has re-opened and he is bleeding from it. All odds seem against him.

But he is encouraged by a note he has received from Iris that confirms what we have been suspecting. Her young son is also Roy's son, who was conceived on their last night together. The note announces that their son is at the game, watching his Dad. This steels Roy's resolve and his true grit prevails.

He takes aim at the last pitch and drills it high into one of the floodlights, breaking it into a thousand brilliant pieces. All sorts of wonderful things begin to happen. The electrical system in the park goes berserk. The powerful bulbs in the flood lights break, sending incandescent showers over Roy as he circles the bases. The dark-windowed office of the criminal cabal is penetrated by the light of the fireworks. The sparks seem to scatter its members like termites who cannot stand the light. Roy wins, the team wins, Pop Fisher wins. The forces of darkness are vanquished. The Knights will remain under the ownership and leadership of Pop Fisher.

Pop tells Roy, "You're the best hitter I've ever seen. Baseball fans will always remember you." Roy's son, along with millions of teenagers, adulate him. The baseball that was prodigiously hit by Roy in the deciding game finally lands. With it we are carried back to a farm in Nebraska. Iris and his son are there with him. Everything is beautiful and peaceful. The story ends where it began, except that Roy's promise has been fulfilled.

He has land, wife, and son. He has proved to himself and others that he is the best. He has struggled upward against heavy odds and prevailed with the virtues that have made America great. He has become a model for others, especially his son. The future has rewarded his efforts; it has finally graciously embraced him. The American Dream has been fulfilled.

Reflections

It is not necessary to dwell too long on interpretation. Roy's life has powerfully duplicated and illustrated the American story. He was formed in the wholesome but lowly American countryside. Reverberations of Eden and Adam redound. But he must shake free of the limits of his past, no matter how wonderful it is. He engages in a struggling ascent. There are at least nine major challenges to his ascent which he must overcome. He does this through his own efforts, though the almost supernatural appearance of his sweetheart (the lady in white) is an important aid. She reintroduces him to the wholesome values he had from his youthful beginnings. Finally, he succeeds. The future embraces him graciously. The Old Testament promise of land and sons is his. Moreover, he has proved himself the best and has become a model for others.

Other related themes are present in the film. America and its virtues win out over the vices of old Europe (Gus Spanos and Memo Paris are representative of unamerican urban vice.) Willed destiny wins out over fate. Harriet Bird, Gus Spanos and Memo Paris all epitomize a "Greek" view of life in which tragic fate harshly limits heroic efforts. America is different. The future is open; it can be willed. Further, there is the celebration of the virtues of rural and small town life over the darkness and evil of the city. The righteousness embodied in those virtues will bring success. The Protestant Ethic's correlation of righteousness and success is firmly in place.

All of these elements—the American story and these related themes—combine to make a powerful statement. Viewers often cheer when Roy hits his final homerun. There is great satisfaction when his struggling ascent is finally blessed. The plot moves along the lines suggested by the American story. The character is the epitome of American virtue. Also, the attitude of the director toward the story he portrays is one of great affection. The care taken to evoke the feelings of American life are impressive and effective. The mythic atmosphere serves to heighten and dramatize the crucial moments in the American story. All things are possible in America. Indeed, the Arthurian legends are most likely to happen in America.

The American Difference

The differences between the American story and the Old Testament narrative have already been briefly described above. Now is an opportune time for a more careful comparison and contrast of the American story with the Christian story, which we examined in detail in Chapter Three.

First, there is a major difference between the American hero and the Christian protagonist with regard to character. The American character has no disastrous internal flaw, no destructive interior bondage, as does the Christian. The American tends, like Roy Hobbs, toward a wholesome but naive innocence. He is not bound by an inevitable inward condition as is the Christian. Therefore, when confronted by serious challenges, which in the American story are more external than internal, the American character does not come under severe judgment, either from himself or others or God. Nor does he accuse himself in a recognition scene precipitated by the judgment of the Law, as does Mack Sledge in *Tender Mercies* or Frank Galvin in *The Verdict*.

Christian characters are more complex and internally jagged than the American. Mack Sledge and Frank Galvin are far more interesting than Roy Hobbs; they certainly have more depth. Therefore, we tend to identify with the Christian characters in their moments of judgment and grace, while we tend to admire and enjoy the American's success after so much struggle on his part. The American hero provides a model that we might want to emulate by exertion of the will; the Christian serves more as the vivid illustration of deep movements of the soul that happen to us, that we receive rather than achieve. The American hero succeeds by his own virtue; the Christian is transformed by grace from outside herself.

With regard to plot, the American hero, like Roy Hobbs, starts from a lowly but basically decent environment, often accompanied by great natural beauty. The Christian starts internally bound but his external conditions may be positive or negative. External conditions are not paramount at the beginning of the Christian story. External conditions might be ideal, like the sumptuous north-shore suburbs of *Ordinary People*, or miserable, like the ramshackle conditions of *Tender Mercies*.

The middle of the American story is loaded with external challenges. There are at least nine of them in Roy Hobbs' struggling ascent. They test the inner strength of the character. In the Christian drama the primary testing is internal; the processes of the plot occasion deep self-examination by the character. The middle of the story is more one of judgment on and forgiveness of the Christian's sin, rather than a set of challenges to her virtue. The American, like Roy Hobbs' lift from the lady in white, may get important strokes of support from those outside him. But the Christian needs more than support in the middle of the Christian story. She needs grace of a liberating sort; she needs the grace event. And this comes in spite of the fact that she is undeserving and it brings forth an internal revolution of the spirit. In the American story, the support comes to bolster the capacities that are already there but need a good nudge. Again, the middle of the American story tends to be focused on the action of the hero—his struggling ascent. The Christian drama focuses on the reception of judgment and grace by the protagonist that may not change her external situation, but changes radically her **relation** to that situation.

The end of the American story is an unambiguously happy one. The providential future embraces the struggle. The Old Testament promise of land and sons is bestowed. While the American has in some sense **earned** his reward, there is also an sense that the blessing is given by the gracious and open future. The Christian experiences new life toward the end of the story, thus becoming through the Spirit active and intentional with her life. The action comes from the dynamic **reunion** of the Christian character with herself, others and the Ground of Being at the middle of the story. The end is an effect of the middle in the Christian story. In the American it is a reward for or a blessing on what has gone on before. Further, the end of the American story presents a pleasant, indeed, blessed external situation for the hero. The end of the Christian story may or may not be successful in the external sense. But the character is living out her new life in that situation, whether or not it is pleasant or happy.

The viewer's response to the unfolding of the American story is suspense during the struggle, admiration for the pluck of the character and elation at his success. The viewers response to the Christian drama is judgment of the internal flaw, forgiveness of the character's sin, and joy in her new life.

The atmosphere of the American story emphasizes the possibilities that life and history can, and most likely will, be blessed by providence. If there is a miracle it has to do with external events. The Christian atmosphere emphasizes the internal miracles of judgment and grace, but does not deny the possibilities of positive historical change wrought by judgment, grace, and new life in human history.

The American Nightmare

From the very beginning of American history there have been dissenters from the optimism of the American Dream. They have often been Christians whose sense of human sin and of the need for divine grace set them apart from the buoyant hope of ascent so prominent in the American story. Hawthorne and Melville, for example, wrote important novels exposing the dark side of human life in America. There has been a long tradition of dramatists—Eugene O'Neill, Arthur Miller, Tennessee Williams, to name several—who challenge the optimism of the American story. In fact, as we come closer to the present day the preponderant number of novelists and dramatists seem to join the party of dissent. However, the best of them probe the mixture of darkness and light that is American life. Only a few are alienated completely from the American story.

As our dramatists and novelists have gone, so have our movie makers. In fact, many famous plays and novels of this sort have found their way onto the screen. *Long Day's Journey Into Night*, *Death of a Salesman*, and *Cat on a Hot Tin Roof* are plays by O'Neill, Miller, and Williams, respectively, that have been adapted for the screen. Each of them reveals through film quite a different vision of life in America than the classic American Dream.

These films reveal graphically not the American Dream but rather the American Nightmare. In some cases the Dream is found wanting because it obscures the truth about life in America. People simply do not engage in the successful struggling ascent that the Dream proposes. Only a few are lucky enough to move upward, and that is at the expense of the many. Classic movies such as *Grapes of Wrath*, as well as others that focus on the struggles of the underdog, contrast the painful futility of the downtrodden with the unmerited luxury of the fat cats. In these cases the Dream itself is not so much attacked as exposed for its lack of honesty about American life.

But the lion's share of American Nightmare movies challenge the intrinsic meaning of the Dream itself. Movies such as the three mentioned above, and more recent films like *Wallstreet, Network, Nashville,* and *The Godfather,* to name a few, are cases in point.

Since the social and political upheaval of the 1960s such movies have increased dramatically. That period in our national life exemplified a severe challenge to the American story. Instead of an Edenic background for the protagonist, there is misery or oppression. Instead of a wholesome, innocent Adam of a character, the protagonist is an anti-hero. He is driven by base motives.

Further, the character either ascends by dishonest and rapacious striving (he doesn't play by the rules), or does not ascend at all because he cannot or will not. In fact, descent in the face of daunting challenges and weakened will are the order of the day.

The future, far from being gracious and open, is threatening, confused and finally closed. Land is lost or never gained and sons either disappoint or do not appear. In short, the Dream has become a Nightmare. As Willy Loman's son, Biff, says at Willy's funeral, "He had all the wrong dreams."

It is interesting to speculate about the causes of this great reversal. Why do so many of our movies now portray an American Nightmare instead of an American Dream? Part of this trend may be attributable to fairly superficial causes—it's easier in this more cynical age to portray ignoble characters caught up in horrific plots than to portray noble characters in uplifting stories. A jaded and cynical viewership is entertained more by the former than the latter.

But there are more profound reasons for the reversal. Certainly one of these is the deep ambiguity in the American Dream itself. Its assertions about human nature and destiny, as well its values of freedom, initiative and natural opportunity, capture only partial truths about the human story. American Nightmare movies depict the consequences of life lived only according to the values celebrated in the American story. While their critique is often exaggerated and fails to affirm sufficiently the values in the American Dream, there is an important correction going on. Arthur Miller pronounces judgment on a life like Willy Loman's that was driven by "all the wrong dreams."

Another consequential reason for the emergence of Nightmare movies is the rise of many sorts of "adversarial cultures" in America, particularly after the upheaval of the sixties. The "normative" culture of America, shaped by the middle-class, white, Christian, Protestant version of the American Dream, was fractured in that upheaval. The coherence of American culture was sharply qualified. Those groups and subcultures on the outside of the "normative" culture have repeatedly asserted their critique of the Dream and, with far less frequency and cogency, proposed alternatives. Most of the time the Nightmare movies preponderantly denounce—often doctrinairely but sometimes profoundly so.

It is in the context of these deep cultural changes that my young students find so much joy in *The Natural*. That movie is a straightforward affirmation of the American Dream in a society that no longer believes in such unambiguous affirmations. Perhaps the young long for the retrieval of cultural myths that are more uplifting and wholesome than the regular fare. Their approval of *The Natural* is matched by their disapproval of *Easy Rider*, which I use as a powerful example of the American Nightmare. (I also use *Easy Rider* as an illustration of the skeptical movie, which I will deal with in Chapter 6.)

Part of their negative reaction to *Easy Rider* has to do with the extended "drug trips" so *de rigueur* in the movies made in the sixties (1965-75) era. But part of it can be understood as the contemporary generation's reluctance to accept such a negative appraisal of the American experience. Nevertheless, the portrayal of the American Nightmare remains an important story running along side the American Dream. A closer look at *Easy Rider* is important for that reason alone.

The American Nightmare in Film: *Easy Rider*

This movie, which enjoys something of a cult status, is Peter Fonda's most important contribution to American film. After its run, he seems to have nearly disappeared from the industry. Perhaps his fate has something to do with the message of the movie, which is bleak, to say the least.

The central figures are Wyatt (Peter Fonda) and Billy (Dennis Hopper). Wyatt is called Captain America and uses the American flag symbolically on his motorcycle and helmet, both of these being rather self-conscious efforts to correlate Wyatt and Billy's story with the story of America. Instead of coming from wholesome and bucolic backgrounds, they are vaguely from the Los Angeles area. When asked directly where they are from, their response is: "It's hard to say; all cities are pretty much alike."

They certainly do shake free from the limits of the past, though their past is definitely not the wholesome but lowly pattern in the American Dream. Their past is more accurately characterized by financial limitations. They have not been able to do what they want—spring free from the day-to-day grind and go on a motorcycle journey across America from West to East, an interesting reversal of most "journey" movies. They also move from decadent and cosmopolitan West Coast culture toward "straight" and parochial Southern culture. Neither place is an apt location for experiencing the American Dream, though the South fiercely claims allegiance to the Dream, often in spite of the experience of many ordinary Southerners.

The movie begins with the sale of drugs by Wyatt and Billy to a fat cat at the foot of a runway at the Los Angeles airport. Wyatt and Billy have purchased the drugs from a Mexican connection and they sell them at a huge profit to a rich Anglo distributor. Wyatt (Captain America) stashes the money in the gas tank of his motorcycle and off the two go on a meandering journey across America. It is clear that the two are not playing by the rules of the American Dream. They sell drugs and they use drugs. Their journey is thus fueled by illicit means. Their behavior is certainly not an attractive model for others to emulate.

Their trip across America is accompanied by a sound track of rock music. The lyrics are something of a commentary on their journey. "No one cares if you live or die" is one song's observation. "God damn the pusher" is another, an ironic comment on Captain America's behavior. The famous "Born to Be Wild" by the Doors provides another illuminating statement.

Everything they do flies in the face of the normative culture of the American Dream. Wyatt throws his watch away; the two will not observe the discipline of time that makes for success in the middle-class world. They are both dressed as hippies and wear long hair. Both smoke marijuana heavily. Billy is more obsessive in his drug use; Wyatt more coolly intentional. Indeed, Wyatt is the one who pushes drugs on others in a seductive way.

Neither participates in the struggling ascent of the American Dream. Billy seems unable. His mind is addled by drugs. He is hyperactive and unstable. What can he do but "go with the flow?" Wyatt obviously could participate in the American ascent. He is intelligent, capable, attractive, calm and collected. He is Captain America. But he refuses to play the game. He wishes neither to participate in the upward ascent nor play by the rules of the game. He rejects discipline, self-sacrifice, a future orientation—the "straight" world of the American story. He is the reverse mirror image of *The Natural*.

Even the American outdoors that they traverse seems equivocal. Sometimes it is grand and beautiful. Other times dark and vaguely sinister. And it is cluttered with derelict buildings and machinery. America is not simply beautiful.

Early in their journey, which now has New Orleans as a penultimate goal, they stop at a Mexican-American family's farm. They are invited to dinner. There a wholesome, straight American family goes through the classic American ritual of prayer and hospitality. Wyatt and Billy seem to respect their way of life. "You should be proud," they tell the farmer. But they must be on their way and off they go. The meeting with this wholesome and friendly family is the only positive encounter with "normal Americans" the two have in the whole movie. After this things move decidedly downward.

However, the next stop gives a glimmer of hope for them that then turns sour. They follow up a tip from a friend and find a commune out in the middle of nowhere. At first the movie portrays the commune hopefully. All the members are physically attractively yet highly unconventional. No one is dressed like an ordinary American. Free love seems to be a distinct possibility. Pot and health food are the order of the day. The commune is attempting a thorough-going natural way of life. Everything about it is countercultural. Wyatt pronounces a benediction upon it: "They're going to make it." Billy and Wyatt slip off with two attractive women for skinny-dipping in a secluded pond. Here indeed are the reverberations of Eden.

But all is not well. The men in the commune cast dark looks at both guests, particularly Billy. Intimations of violence toward them lurk ominously amid the sunny climate. One of the women tries to get Wyatt to stay. "This may be the time and place," she says. But it cannot be. They are outsiders, and will remain so. Billy and Wyatt leave quickly, one step ahead of some calamity that they intensely sense. The commune no longer seems so attractive, even to the viewer.

Events continue to move downward. They ride into a small town during a parade. They playfully ride between the orderly rows of the high school band, contrasting their hippy individuality with the regimentation of the young marchers. The town police are not amused; they throw the two in jail. There they meet one George Hanson (played by the young Jack Nicholson), the disheveled, hung-over son of a wealthy and well-connected family in town. Though a lawyer, George seems to use his skills only for getting himself out of jail after his binges.

He is obviously not happy with his life, nor are his parents. His mother saved his football helmet to give to his own son, but George is neither married nor likely to be. He, like Wyatt and Billy, is in rebellion from the demands of the American Dream. On the spur of the moment, George decides to leave his sodden life in that small town and join the other two on their journey. His exit is accompanied by the song "I wanna be a bird."

George's liberation proceeds. He is offered a joint by Captain America and it blows his mind. He is promised more potent stuff later. Around their campfire he waxes philosophically. He observes that this used to be a good country where freedom was a real possibility, but such freedom is no longer allowed. He tells Wyatt and Billy that they represent real freedom and that is threatening to the hypocritical and oppressive society they now have to live in. They are dangerous because they are really free.

The three have already had near-violent encounters with the Southerners they meet. Even going into a cafe in their garb is a provocative act. After one such encounter in which young girls are attracted to the trio, the locals act. They attack the trio's camp in the middle of the night. They beat the three with bats and clubs. George is killed.

The other two flee in terror. They don't even bother to notify George's parents about his death. They press on to New Orleans and Mardi Gras. Interestingly, Mardi Gras has roots in the religious tradition of one last fling before Lent. It is their last fling.

Mardi Gras itself is frightening. Grotesque characters seem to menace the two. The atmosphere of New Orleans is nightmarish. Wyatt takes Billy to a brothel recommended by some friends back in Los Angeles. Billy eagerly anticipates the coming sexual encounter. Wyatt is unmoved by lust. He coolly selects a partner and heads out into the streets. They find their way to a cemetery where Wyatt slips his partner, who is named Mary, a dose of LSD. He also partakes.

A terrible trip for both unfolds. There is a cacophony of singing voices. The Apostles' Creed and the Lord's Prayer are accompanied by obscene and monstrous images of sex and violence. A vision of the Virgin Mary brings forth an anguished cry from Wyatt: "Cruel mother, I hate you so much." Wyatt's tortured but hidden past is revealed. The cool character is deeply tormented, and he is willing to foist his own torment on the unsuspecting prostitute. Hired sex would have been a better bargain for her.

The bad drug trip subsides and we find the two friends on the road again, aimlessly drifting into an evermore dangerous future. On their last night Wyatt reflects on their journey as the two sit smoking dope around their campfire. His simple summary is: "We blew it."

But this realization doesn't stop their inexorable movement toward violent death. The next day they are riding down a rural road when they meet two country rubes in a pick-up with a shot-gun rack in the back window. (Southern country folk always seem to be an easy and risk-free target for Hollywood stereotyping. *Easy Rider* is full of such clichés.)

The two hicks decide to get themselves some hippies. They turn their pick-up around and pursue Billy and Wyatt.

Billy is shot first. His bike crashes and Wyatt frantically goes to his aid. It's too late and Wyatt finally loses his cool. The pick-up returns to finish the job. The film ends with the two dead by their bikes. A river flows to the sea in the background.

This story obviously stands the American Dream on its head. The characters and the plot are reverse mirror images of the classic American story. There is no Eden in America and the land is not populated by Adams. There is no struggling ascent according to the rules. Both characters reject such a trajectory and adopt a lifestyle opposed to it. But that leads to a dark and dangerous future where life is lost. Land and sons are not even a possibility, let alone the shalom that is part of the promise of America. The Dream is a bad one. Indeed, the very atmosphere of America is nightmarish.

Yet, the director of the film, Fonda himself, does not seem to endorse the kind of rebellion represented by Billy and Wyatt. They are no more attractive than the "ordinary" Americans they meet on their journey. The self-imposed judgment on their actions is clear: we blew it. Both the American Dream and active rebellion from it seem to be equally destructive, and the film suggests no real alternative. Farm life of an ordinary sort and life in a rural commune are the only positive notes in the movie, but even they are no real possibility for ordinary Americans. The movie leaves us in despair.

While *Easy Rider* may be a rather extreme example of the American nightmare, there is no shortage of similar statements. I have listed a number of them above and in an appendix. The continuing appearance of strong statements of both the American Dream and the American Nightmare reveals the ongoing argument about the meaning of America. Perhaps we need more treatments of the American vision that deal with the full ambiguity—the real highs and lows—of our national existence.

Chapter 5

The Greek Story

The number of Greek stories in popular feature length movies is small. There are no happy endings, as in the American story. There are no moving transformations of character that typify the Christian story. Indeed, the fate of the tragic hero is grim. Such austere attributes no doubt sentence Greek movies to minority status. Unsurprisingly, most Greek films are Anglo-European in origin, not American.

Yet, the vision of life shaped by the Greek philosophers and tragenians of antiquity stubbornly persists, even in current popular films.[16] It also persists in drama and philosophy, witness the continuing presence of the Greek heritage in theaters and university classrooms around the world. The vision the Greeks forged is too profound and compelling for it to disappear. It is perennial. In movies like *Breaker Morant* and *The Boat*, that vision is powerfully presented in today's films.

The Greek Story

It is perhaps best to start our explication of the Greek story with the narrative element we have termed "atmosphere," though such an order of discussion will scramble things a bit. We have used "atmosphere" to refer to the boundaries, limits, and conditions which surround human life. Atmosphere has to do with the background conditions—both proximate and ultimate—that make the plot move in the way it does and which in turn presents the crucial challenges to the characters involved in the plot.

The Greek atmosphere is affected by the Greek notion of God, especially that of the classical philosophers. To them God is transcendent, unmoved, self-sufficient, impersonal, unchanging, and eternal. Further, God is impassible, unaffected by and uninvolved with persons in the world of nature and history. Such involvement would destroy God's divinity. God is the "Unmoved Mover" of Aristotle or the eternal forms of the Good, True, and Beautiful of Plato. God is pure reason, perfect intelligence.

Unfortunately, this God of the philosophers, though the unconditioned ground of the Good, has no will or ability to work out that good in human life and history. However, the gods of Greek religion do have personality and will. These gods, very different from the God of the philosophers, behave much like humans, though with more power. There are many of them and they control much of what happens in this life and this history. Unfortunately, they are capricious and arbitrary as well as jealous. In fact, they are in a highly competitive relationship with humans. When Prometheus tries to steal the fire of the gods, they strike him down. They hover in the background of the Greek story, waiting to destroy the achievements of mortal human beings. They control the fate of every human being, and they are not friendly. Indeed, the gods of life and history are fate.

These two divergent images of divinity have something very important in common. Neither possesses any empathy with human aspirations. The gods of Greek religion are too selfish to take seriously the cry of the human spirit. Though the God of the philosophers is the ground of the Good, True, and Beautiful, which humans as rational creatures can recognize and pursue, that God does nothing to help them in their pursuit. Further, when intelligent human beings do exercise their divine reason in life and history, they make the gods of Greek religion jealous and angry. Those gods move to strike down the pretensions of the merely human. Such is the painful predicament of the Greek tragic hero. He participates in the divine through his intelligence but his efforts to exercise it in this bodily and historical life are bound to come to naught.

These are the background conditions of human life shaped by Greek philosophy and theology. The Greek dramatists, permeated by these notions from Greek philosophy and religion, created the most penetrating articulations of this human predicament in their tragedies.

The Greek tragic hero participates in the divine essence, reason. He, like God, seems strangely complete in himself. He is intellectual, sensitive. His inherent nobility, however, is imprisoned in his body. His life, furthermore, must submit to history, in which he is inescapably enmeshed. While noble and internally free, he is externally bound. Essentially helpless in his bodily, historical existence, he cannot escape his fate.

As a bodily being, the main character in the Greek story has passions and feelings. He does not always allow his reason to guide his actions. Further, he may be complacent about or ignorant of a threatening situation. These weaknesses may constitute his tragic flaw. Either through the exercise of passion or ignorance, the tragic hero makes a fateful mistake for which the gods make him pay. The Greek character's flaw, however, is not the internal bondage of sin. Its exercise does not lead to religious or moral guilt, but it does lead to doom.

This brings us to the plot in a Greek story. At the beginning of a Greek story, there seems to be a hint that the character is free to shape his destiny. But there is already something problematic about that freedom; the character is already enmeshed in events that are threatening. Through flashbacks or reveries we are shown the noble qualities of the character. He is intelligent and accomplished; he has mastered many of the ennobling practices of human life. He has the capacity to flourish. Even at the beginning, however, we are aware that all is not well with him; he is caught up in events beyond his control. The appearance of external freedom is illusory.

As the plot proceeds, his involvement in the inexorable movement of fate becomes more threatening. Daunting challenges confront him. Under their pressure, he makes an error of judgment or passion. He acts or fails to act without knowing the full consequences of his action or failure to act. Or he allows his passions to lead to dangerous and neglectful deeds even in the face of known consequences. Or his ignorance and passion together combine to lead to self-destructive repercussions. At any rate, his tragic deed leads to a terrible reversal of fortune. Events catch up with him and bring him to impending doom.

In the midst of these threatening events, he, in a moment of retrospective reflection, recognizes the tragic act that has taken place earlier. The bitterness of truth descends upon him; he has acted wrongly (rashly or unwisely) and will pay a price for that act far in excess of its offensiveness. The further playing out of events will bring doom, no matter what he does now. He is caught.

At the end of the story, the Greek tragic hero nobly defies or accepts the necessity of fate. His defiance and/or acceptance are "fitting"; instead of detracting from the inner nobility of the character, they enhance it. The time before the final end (which is often but not always violent) is characterized by suffering nobility. We generally observe this in moments of quiet contemplation when the character shows an inner serenity and self-sufficiency. There may be weariness or melancholy, but never panic or frenzy before his impending doom. The Greek tragic hero maintains his composure to the end.

Doom does occur. The tragic act that stemmed from the tragic flaw brings ineluctable consequences. The life, achievements or loved ones of the hero are lost. Fate has exacted its harsh penalty.

The effects of the Greek story on the viewer are states of both fear and pity. Greek tragedy brings forth fear that life has this remorseless quality to it, that life brings down even the most noble among us. It also elicits pity for the character, for the consequences of his misdeed are far out of proportion to the moral guilt incurred. Yet there is a deep admiration for the nobility he sustains in the fateful course of events.

The creator of the story usually has the same attitude toward the story as the viewer. Fear, pity and admiration are accompanied by a bitter realism about the doomed fate of human excellence.

The Greek Story in Film : *Breaker Morant*

As already noted, the Greek story appears only infrequently in films, for obvious reasons. But such films are made; and they are often made well. Knowing from the beginning that the films will not be overwhelming successes at the box office, the creators of the movies do not make compromises to popular taste. *Breaker Morant, The Boat*, already mentioned, and *Gallipoli* and *The Eagle Has Landed* are several films that come to mind. For some reason, Australian movie-makers seem to have a penchant for the Greek story. *Breaker Morant*, for example, was done by Bruce Beresford, an Australian director. Let us take a closer look at this fine movie.

The movie is set in South Africa at the time of the Boer War. The British are locked in a new and dirty kind of warfare with the Boers. This particular war marks the beginnings of guerilla warfare. The war is winding down and the British want a peace conference. Above all, they don't want the Germans, who are sympathetic with the Boers, to enter the war. Thus, they want to impress all parties with their just dealings and peaceful intentions, even though they have been guilty of setting up horrible concentration camps and of summarily executing Boer guerillas.

The movie begins with the trial of three members of the Bushfield Carabiniers, an Australian military unit. The leader of the three is Lt. Harry "Breaker" Morant (Edward Woodward), a strong, handsome and dignified man. His compatriots are Col. Peter Hancock, a soldier out of economic necessity, and the young George Whitton, an idealist who has volunteered to fight "for the glory of the empire." The three are charged with summarily shooting Boer prisoners and with the murder of a German missionary, the Rev. Hess. The three participated in these killings, so it seems, to avenge the ambush death of their much beloved leader, Captain Hunt.

As the trial is being readied, we are transported to Kitchener's palace some distance away, where the British brass are talking about the trial. We begin to get a glimpse of the difficulties the Aussies are going to face. The British speak with contempt about "the colonials" (the Australians) and their legendary lack of discipline. For the sake of prospects for peace, they think it would be good if the Australians were executed. This would show British commitment to humane rules of warfare and signal their desire for a peaceful conclusion to a very nasty war. By punishing the Aussies for the killing of Rev. Hess, they would smooth the ruffled feathers of the Germans who had been threatening to intervene. Further, by showing an upright sense of justice on these relatively isolated offenses, they might avoid more serious charges surrounding the systematic use of concentration camps for Boer women and children, camps in which thousands of non-combatants have died.

Back to the trial. The Aussies are assigned a lawyer, a Major Thomas (Jack Thompson), who turns out to be totally inexperienced in trial law. He doesn't know which end is up. The powers-that-be are making sure that the Aussies don't have a chance. The prisoners see their prospects for winning acquittal dim considerably.

As the trial proceeds, we are given glimpses of the defendants lives before the war. "Breaker," Lt. Morant's nickname, comes from his ability to break wild horses. We also find out that he is a man of great literary sensibility—he reads, recites, and writes poetry. He also sings well enough to entertain at small concerts. He was also engaged to a beautiful woman, Captain Hunt's sister. All in all, as a Greek tragic hero, he is accomplished and noble. He is a man of great excellence whose capacities lift him far above the raucous squalor of the war and its jejune trial. Moreover, he is a man of contemplation who can savor these excellences in an utterly self-sufficient way. He doesn't need the support of others, though he is certainly not unfriendly or aloof.

Perhaps the most meaningful relationship of his life was his friendship with Captain Hunt, which in true Greek fashion, was a friendship among equally noble men. We find out in a flashback about the death of Captain Hunt. He led what he thought was a surprise attack on a camp of Boer guerillas. However, the Boers had been forewarned by a spy within the Australian ranks. Captain Hunt was wounded, captured, tortured, killed, and mutilated by the Boers.

Morant leads a party to track down the offending Boers. When they catch them Morant notices with rising anger that one of the prisoners is wearing Captain Hunt's jacket. Then he quickly orders the immediate execution of the captives. Several friends counsel prudence, but Morant reminds them of the current practice of taking no prisoners. Hunt himself had executed prisoners and the higher brass had actually issued a rule allowing such executions, in view of the fact that the Empire forces had no facilities for keeping prisoners in this new kind of mobile war.

Nevertheless, Breaker does act rashly out of his anguish over losing his friend. He fatefully engages in an act of passion, which, in the normal course of events would not have even been noticed. But he is enmeshed in a series of events over which he has no control. He doesn't even know of the British intention to make an example of some poor colonials for the sake of greater goods—peace and the good reputation of the British. Someone has to be the scapegoat and the three Aussies are selected, whether or not they are really guilty at all.

Even with their decreasing odds, however, the Aussies fight back. The inexperienced Major Thomas begins to act like a real lawyer. He essentially proves to the military court that Morant was not breaking the normal rules of engagement. His skilled argument shows that the Bushfield Carabiniers, far from being undisciplined and murderous, were well-led and innocent of the very charges that the British would like to attach to them. Further, he demonstrates that the Rev. Hess was not an innocent by-stander but a German agent who had often tipped off the Boers to British and Australian intentions, resulting in the loss of many soldiers.

In the midst of the trial a Boer contingent actually attacks the military outpost where the trial is being held. We are given the chance to see Breaker in action. Brave, cool, and collected, he leads a defense that turns back the Boers.

Major Thomas makes a moving summary argument before the court. Any fair-minded person would be persuaded that the accused were innocent of anything deserving more than a mild reprimand. But the dice have been thrown. The judges are under instructions to find them guilty. Thomas does not suspect this and predicts an acquittal after the summary arguments have been made.

Breaker knows better. He bitterly recognizes that the game is fixed and that he played into it with the rash decision he made earlier. He knows their fate is sealed. Another officer, aware that the three are basically innocent, offers an escape to Breaker. In Socrates-like fashion he refuses such a way out, but not for Socrates-like reasons. He does not submit himself to the laws of the state out of respect for the state.

Rather, he takes a more Platonic option. He tells the well-meaning officer that he has seen the world. There is nothing that he hasn't seen or done that he any longer wants to see or do. Obviously weary of this bodily life in a capricious history, he is ready to take leave.

He doesn't have to wait long. The next morning the verdicts are given by the military tribunal—death by firing squad for Morant and Hancock, life imprisonment for the young Whitton. Breaker spends the long last evening of his life in contemplation and writing. He is serene and composed. Death holds no terror for him. His mind is already absorbed in something more permanent than frail human life; it is contemplating and creating the Beautiful.

The next morning the two are marched off. Morant refuses the solace of a clergyman. He says he's a pagan even as he quotes Matthew 10:36: "A man's enemies will be the members of his own household." He steadies his friend, Col. Hancock, with his calm dignity, and they march hand-in-hand to their execution. They both refuse blind-folds and stare their executioners in the eye. Breaker's last words are: "Shoot straight; we don't want any mess." After they are shot, their bodies are collected and put into coffins to the ironic strains of "Soldiers of the Queen."

The movie can be taken as a protest against war, as an indictment of colonialism and imperialism, or even as an anti-British polemic on the part of aggrieved "colonials." But I think its Greek themes are unmistakable. Breaker is a noble character who gets enmeshed in a fateful course of events beyond his control which lead inexorably to his doom. He is by far the noblest character in the movie, yet he is made to suffer far out of proportion to the deed he has rashly performed. He becomes fully aware of this fateful necessity and faces his fate with noble but measured defiance. The plain message of the movie is that life is like that. The Greeks had it right. The noble suffer a fateful end.

The Greek Difference

We need not belabor the obvious in charting the differences among the Greek story and its Christian and American counterparts. But a few observations may be helpful in high-lighting the divergences in the way each story handles the elements of narrative.

The atmosphere of the Greek story is hostile to the aspirations of noble human beings for this life. Life is stacked against Breaker. The nobler the character the harder his fall. "The real god of life and history in Greek tragedy is fate, and fate is man's enemy, not man's friend."[17] However, there is the mystic route of escape. Breaker has intelligent capacities that enable him to transcend this portentous existence. He can also enjoy the goods of this life with the kind of detachment necessary for those who are aware of their limitations.

The Greek atmosphere is decidedly different from the Christian and American. The Christian atmosphere is conditioned by belief in a divine presence in history that brings characters through judgment to redemption and new life. " Life and history are redeemable in principle and in part redeemed at certain crucial moments in fact."[18] The American story posits a providential future that embraces the American hero who shakes free from the limits of the past and engages in a struggling ascent.

The Greek tragic character, like the American, is not substantially qualified or transformed by his involvement in the processes of history. Lt. Morant is noble from the beginning and remains unflinchingly noble to the end. In the Greek vision, moreover, such nobility of character is rare. Most humans simply do not possess it. The American character is determined to reach success from the beginning and has the fortitude and discipline to win. The American character may be strengthened by his challenges but not transformed. It is the Christian character who begins with an internal bondage that necessitates liberation from resources outside herself. She needs both judgment and grace.

The Greek plot moves from a glimmer of freedom and hope at the beginning. We have hope that Breaker will be extricated from his predicament. For a while it looks like that might happen. Certainly it should happen. But there is no real openness; there is an inexorable move toward doom. The glimmer of freedom is illusory; Breaker's life is irredeemable in principle. Midway in the plot the tragic flaw (Breaker's passionate act of vengeance) leads to his downfall and he recognizes this in a bitter moment after the act. From there on his demise is inevitable.

The American plot moves upward instead of downward. Though they are certainly not painless, the challenges in the middle of the story are finally surmounted on the way to a happy ending. The plot of the Christian story is perhaps the most complex. The beginning is one of internal bondage, the middle one of judgment and grace, and the end one of new life in the midst of a continuing challenges.

The qualities of character and the movement of plot, it seems, are dependent upon the fundamental background assumptions of the narrative, its atmosphere. The Greek conception of the ultimate reality in which we live, move and have our being, is one that is basically out to get us. The American presumes that virtues of freedom, initiative, and determination will out. There is something at the heart of reality—providence—that will finally reward virtue with happiness. The Christian atmosphere assumes a divine presence and action that challenges characters in the midst of their sin, redeems them through grace, and enables a new life of faith, love, and hope. In all three cases there is a power, an intentional presence, that makes the plot move in the way it does. Their ontological background imposes a meaningful direction on the plot.

The creator of the narrative has a similar posture towards it that the viewer is likely to have in response. Great respect for noble human beings is fitting in the Greek case, with fear and pity for their eventual fate. Admiration for the determined hero is demanded in the American case, with happiness that providence blesses such determination. Judgment and forgiveness is appropriate for the Christian story, with a joy for the new life that follows. Each of these three stories invites us to enter into them, reflecting on whether they illuminate what happens to us in the experience of our lives, on what greater reality we confront, and on what kind of lives we, in the face of these meanings, should live.

Chapter 6

The Skeptical Story

The Skeptical Story in a Skeptical World

The Christian, American, and Greek stories place the human drama within a context that gives each human story meaning. There is "something out there" with which the human contends. This "something" conditions heavily what the shape and direction of the plot will be. In the three stories we have already covered, there is an active, transcendent, meaningful, presence in life and history to which humans respond. In the Christian and American stories that presence, God, is finally affirmative of human aspiration. In contrast, the Greek story points to a presence, fate, that tragically frustrates or destroys human aspiration. But in all three cases, the story can make sense because human subjects encounter something meaningful—even if negative—beyond themselves. In other words, the background atmosphere of these three kinds of narratives gives meaning to both character and plot.

Such is not the case with the skeptical story. There is no meaning bestowed on the human drama by its ultimate context, since that is itself neutral, meaningless, or absurd. We definitely turn a corner when we take up the skeptical story in modern movies.

Skepticism is certainly not a new phenomenon in human history. By the fourth century before our common era the Greeks had already explored several skeptical options. Epicurus, Democritus, and the Sophists based their visions of life on the assumption that there was no human-affirming meaning in the universe. Even the Bible has whiffs of skepticism—"vanity of vanities, all is vanity."

Skepticism emerges in powerful form in the radical wing of the Enlightenment of the 18th Century. Atheism becomes a commonplace in the intellectual classes from then on. But, by and large, radical skepticism has played little role in the popular culture of most Western nations; it seems especially absent in American film until recently. The Christian and American stories have held too much sway over ordinary people.

But things have changed. As we argued earlier, the 1960s were a watershed time in American history. The dominant belief in the American Dream was challenged by many powerful currents and events. Other conventional beliefs and behaviors were placed under scrutiny and often revised or rejected. Religious and moral taboos fell. As one commentator put it, "We fell into the abyss of our own possibilities."

One of the possibilities that had been suppressed by various taboos in American life was that of radical skepticism. Popular literature, TV, music, or film were traditionally not the place for exploring the loss of belief in the American or Christian story. But from the mid-sixties onward, skeptical views came to compete with those others in popular culture. Indeed, many of the American nightmare movies were also deeply skeptical in a general sense.

The skeptical story assumes that the ultimate context in which we live is random, absurd, meaningless. No god, either supportive or hostile to human longing, exists. We have nothing to bounce up against. So there is no object of human religious aspiration, nor is there any divine subject of our salvation. Both pious hopes are illusions, projections of human wishes.

The death of God has further repercussions. There is no ontological grounding for morality. There is nothing outside ourselves which confirms our moral standards. Nor is there any guiding hand, visible or invisible, in human history. At best, history reports the fragmented stories of human acts. At worst, it is one damn thing after the other.

This deflation of meaning and value extends to humans too. In all three stories we have covered thus far humans are in some sense images of God. The Greek honors human reason as of divine origin. The Christian and American view humans as created in the image of God. Though fallen, they still have capacity for covenantal relations with God and others. They are given dominion over the earth. In both cases, humans have dignity and worth.

In the skeptical perspective, humans exhibit a kind of lostness and rootlessness in relation to themselves, others, and the universe. Possessing no "image of God," they are free to be what they will. In skeptical stories that freedom leads to ignoble, perverse, or mean inclinations. Awful things issue from these misshapen figures.

The skeptical plot begins with a modicum of hopefulness. Sometimes there is even zest for life or the dream of a wonderful, if somewhat impossible, future. The main characters seem passably normal, but we catch hints that they may be seriously off-center or deformed. Often the characters are haunted by memories—reveries of better times or remembrances of guilty deeds. Later we find out how these memories torment the character and bring out their latent abnormalities.

The skeptical story moves downward from a slightly hopeful beginning. The middle finds the character involved with threatening events and persons that challenge her further. But this pressure point is not like the one that operates in the Christian or American story. It does not press for a repentance that allows the movement of grace. Neither does it test the mettle of American hero nor the nobility of the Greek.

Rather, the pressure point in a skeptical story finally forces a dramatic revelation of the character's full deformity. From that point we know the situation is hopeless for the skeptical anti-hero. She buffets others to and fro and/or gets buffeted to and fro by others as piteously abnormal as she.

The end of the skeptical story can resemble the end of the Greek. A violent end is one common to both skeptical and Greek stories, but there the similarities end. The Greek hero defies or accepts his doom without losing his dignity or nobility. The skeptical anti-hero despairingly precipitates or succumbs to her own end. She becomes weary, worn, melancholy, or even insane. She squanders her life or curses the day she was born. It is a bad end.

Or, in a stunning reversal, the anti-hero may in fact "win." Since there is nothing in nature or history that resists or confirms human acts, there is nothing to prevent "might making right" or vice prevailing. If they play the power game properly, the bad guys may well win at the end of a skeptical story.

A crucial element in understanding the skeptical story is the creator's attitude toward the story, her tone. In two of the stories we have explored thus far, the Christian and the American, the tone of the creator is generally one of approval of the story just told. The two others may take a different posture to their story. For instance, the Greek storyteller may communicate an implicit or explicit protest against cruel fate. The American nightmare's storyteller may show contempt for those who hold the American Dream and approval or ambivalence (as in *Easy Rider*) for those who rebel against it.

But the skeptical storyteller's attitude toward her story is the most varied of all, and the most crucial. The director can simply intend to elicit the response of despair to which the story naturally leads. That is our real, unadorned plight in life, she seems to say.

Or, adopting a very different tone, the teller can portray the skeptical story so shockingly that we turn away from it with disgust. Then we think, and the author no doubt thinks, that there must certainly be something more valuable in the human story than what has been shown. Thus, there is an implicit opening for the Christian, humanist, American, or Greek version of human life. If things can turn out this badly in a life without belief—or without the moral meanings such belief can give, let's consider something else. Such a stance is sometimes taken by Christian, Jewish, or humanist writers. The story they have told under skeptical assumptions becomes a warning to the viewer. Don't follow this path. The movie, *Handful of Dust*, based on a book by Evelyn Waugh, the Catholic writer, moves much along these lines.

However, the director or writer may project an attitude of resignation before the absurdity of human life. If things are really like this, she seems to be saying, it is best to batten down the hatches and carefully pursue one's own bliss. Life does not offer much for free so take what you can get when you can get it. It is too bad that this is the case, but it is. Act accordingly. Thus, in movies in which anti-heroes "win," the creator may justify, however poignantly, their actions.

The Skeptical Story in Film

As one might expect, there are many varieties of skeptical movies. One major kind is represented by one we have already examined. The American Nightmare, though set in America, is often a more general statement about human life and destiny. This is certainly true of *Easy Rider* and *Who's Afraid of Virginia Wolf?* But there are many more skeptical movies that are only incidentally set in an American context, such as *Chinatown* or *They Shoot Horses, Don't They?* Naturally, there are also a host of skeptical movies that are not American in origin or setting. Let us examine three important movies that express the skeptical story about life.

Ironweed

Based on a novel by William Kennedy, *Ironweed* stars Jack Nicholson and Meryl Streep. It is set in Albany, New York, in the late 1930s when the United States was still mired in the Great Depression. Both main characters, Francis Phalen (Jack Nicholson) and Helen Archer (Meryl Streep), are denizens of the vagrant culture of rough and ready Albany. He is an alcoholic, as is she, though her body is by now decrepit and diseased from the ravages of alcohol and life on the street. He is like an ironweed, though, resilient and hard to kill.

Francis hasn't been home to his wife, Annie, and his two children, Bill and Peg, for twenty-two years. He prefers the travelling hobo life in the company of drunken comrades. Later we discover that times were not always like the present. Francis was a promising young baseball player and almost made the big leagues. His glove and several memento baseballs are kept in the attic of his home, as are the suits he wore when he was part of the respectable world. He has good memories of that time.

But he is also haunted by two painful memories. He brashly but accidentally killed a trolley-car driver in the midst of a bitter strike many years ago. Francis was a striking worker; in the process of pelting a group of "scab" transport workers he hits a trolley driver in the forehead with a powerfully-thrown stone. During Francis' drunken binges, the apparitions of the dead driver, as well as another dead hobo he killed later, visit him. They accuse him of wrongfully killing them. He is terrified by them and shouts counter-charges back at them.

The other terrible memory is one that recalls the death of his infant son, Gerald, whom he dropped on his head after drinking heavily. Early on in the movie he visits his son's grave for the first time in many years to ask for forgiveness for taking his life.

Helen is Francis's companion. They have a strong loyalty to one another, though their way of life constantly interrupts any settled relationship. Helen has a tattered elegance that remains from her younger days when she was a promising singer. She, too, was brought up in the respectable world with bright prospects for the future. She often reminds Francis that she "was born to be a star." Indeed, she saves money so she can periodically stay in a decent boarding house, where she listens to fine music on her Victrola and dreams of what might have been. Indeed, the two of them are in a real sense the king and queen of the hobos.

Both characters, then, are burdened by promising pasts that did not turn out the way they should have. In addition, Francis has great deposits of guilt in his past. The present is filled with squalor—living from hand to mouth, drinking heavily, sleeping in the rough, and brawling with other drunks. Helen has to perform sexual favors for disgusting hobos in order to gain minimal shelter from the cold nights. Her body can no longer live up to the challenges of the rough life; she has a nasty cough and serious stomach pains that make it difficult for her to eat.

Yet, they retain a certain dignity and perhaps a capacity to retrieve their lost lives. The early parts of the movie show them both talking about efforts to start anew. There is a glimmer of hope for both. Francis, however, comes closer to a real new beginning than Helen, partly because she seems to have no one besides Francis to offer her the possibility. Francis' prospects are much better. He has his family.

The middle of the story finds the dramatic tension heightening. Francis decides to return home for Thanksgiving. He works for enough money to purchase a turkey to present to his wife when he goes to her door for the first time in twenty-two years. He approaches with understandable trepidation but Annie greets him with surprised affection. She welcomes him home and he responds with humble gratitude. Their home soon becomes a crucible of both affection and accusation.

His son, Bill, like his mother, greets his father with an offer of reconciliation. Bill has a son who is regaled by his grandfather with tales of the old baseball days. His daughter, Peg, however, is not so generous. She reacts with anger to Francis's return, telling him she is "way past forgiveness." Francis is properly contrite in the face of accusations. "I'm mean to everybody and everything," he confesses.

The family prepares for Thanksgiving. Peg softens her judgment of her father. Francis takes a long hot bath and puts on his good clothes. He sleeps in a comfortable bed and wakes up to sunshine streaming through his bedroom window. A new dawn in his life is possible. Everything seems set for his permanent homecoming.

The stage is prepared even further for Francis's restoration. He confesses to his wife his many sins and shortcomings. Annie listens with great sensitivity and then asks him, "What do you need, Frances?" We expect him to say "You and the family," or perhaps "Forgiveness," or even "Another chance."

We are disappointed and shocked with his response. He says, "I need a shoelace." He refuses the chance for restoration and exerts his own stubborn autonomy. His defiant and willful character has been fully revealed. He gets up and walks away to the rear of the house. There an awful vision appears. He sees a choir of somber and accusing ghosts in his back yard singing the *Dies Irae*—the divine judgment section of the Catholic mass. The men he killed are in the front row.

Meanwhile, Helen has been hitting the skids. She can no longer eat and Francis is typically nowhere to be found. She checks into her favorite boarding house where a kindly owner keeps the treasured items she cannot take with her on the street—a phonograph, records of Beethoven's piano concertos, and decent gowns. She bathes, fixes her hair and dresses up. She puts on the Beethoven and dreams of an elegant life full of beauty—one she once thought she would have but no longer can. She dies alone.

Francis is back on the street with his other friends. They welcome him back. He is a confirmed bum and they know it. He shows his loyalty to one young friend by taking him to a hospital after a terrible beating. The friend dies. Francis then goes to the boarding house where he hopes Helen is waiting. He finds her body on the floor. In a tender moment he touches her and says, "You're mighty pretty....I'm gonna get you a gravestone."

But he doesn't. The call of the road beckons and the last scene of the movie finds him in a railcar on the way to nowhere, plagued by alcohol-induced hallucinations of the people he has killed or rejected.

The movie elicits both poignance and despair. Poignance because we are moved by the painful realization that their lives could have been successful. Despair because their characters are irretrievably twisted. They are hard and unyielding. They are ironweed.

The skeptical themes in the movie are too obvious to elaborate here. Character and plot follow the skeptical schema. But what of the atmosphere and of the author's attitude toward the story? The atmosphere, as well as the plot, seem to offer the possibility of redemption, especially for Francis. Morevoer, the director exercises strong judgment of Francis. Helen seems more pathetic than Francis, thus escaping the same kind of judgment.

Could it be that the writer, intentionally or unintentionally, has really written a failed Christian story, or at least a possible Christian story whose main character refuses to accept grace when it is clearly offered? Or, has the author written a parable of human nature, unable to repent and receive grace? Or is it more of a specific judgment of certain kinds of defiant people? Is the movie a meditation on the unforgivable sin of rejecting grace when it is clearly offered? It seems there are no easy answers to these questions, though the overall thrust of the movie seems skeptical.

Blue Velvet

Directed by David Lynch, this movie has become something of a horror classic. It conveys many mixed meanings, which I will later try to sort out, but finally falls, I think, into the skeptical type. It is sufficiently shocking that many persons find it difficult to watch. It has a nightmarish quality about it.

It starts with a seemingly idyllic scene in a small American town, Lumberton. Kids play, flowers abound, and friendly policemen greet citizens on neat streets bowered with luxuriant trees. It's all red, white, and blue. It seems like a movie devoted to the American Dream. Yet, it seems plastic and phony. The flowers seem false and the people act like robots. The cozy peace is an illusion.

The illusion is shattered as the camera pans in on a man watering his lawn. The hose breaks, the man falls down with a stroke, and his dog barks frantically. Near the fallen man the camera gives us a glimpse of an opening in the churning earth. Beneath its surface bugs are busy attacking and devouring one another. There is a veritable maelstrom of frightening and chaotic struggles going on right under the grass. This is a taste of things to come.

The stricken man's son, Jeffrey Beaumont, goes to the hospital to see his father, who can no longer speak. On the way he crosses a derelict plot of land where he finds a severed human ear. The background is filled with unpleasant and ominous noises of insects feeding upon one another.

Jeffrey is slightly shocked but also intrigued by his find. He dutifully takes the ear to the local police. The detective in charge, Det. Williams, who is the father of Jeffrey's girlfriend, meets Jeffrey's disturbing find with curious detachment and flatness. He seems less than eager to follow the case up, but tells Jeffrey he will do so.

That night Jeffrey meets his girlfriend, Sandy. He tells her of his weird experience and she imparts some privileged information she has as the chief detective's daughter. She tells Jeffrey that the ear may have some connection with a case currently being investigated by the police. It seems that the husband of a local singer, Dorothy Valens, is missing, and that she has an ongoing relationship with a known criminal, Frank Booth. Both items have aroused some police suspicion and they are looking into them, Sandy tells Jeffrey.

As they converse on a dark street, we are again given another fearsome view into the malevolence lurking behind ordinary reality. It is a pitch-black night, the trees have demonic shapes and sway threateningly in the wind, and ominous music swells in the background. We know something evil is afoot.

Jeffrey begins to reveal his personality in his conversation with Sandy. He wants to go see the singer's apartment. Sandy knows the address and he coaxes her to reveal it. He seems obsessively curious. He tells her he wants to take every opportunity for knowledge and experience, even if it involves risk. Sandy is upset by this but consents to go along with the scheme he cooks up.

He poses as a pest control expert to gain entrance to the singer's apartment. He successfully steals her key and plots to break into her apartment later in the evening.

While Jeffrey is convincing the reluctant Sandy to be a lookout for him when he breaks in, we are given a look at Dorothy Valen's performance at the Slow Club, a local night club. The only song we hear is her rendition of "Blue Velvet," a song made popular in the 70s by Bobby Darren. The song, I believe, is really a pop version of an old Polish melody. It is a romantic, nostalgic song given a haunting twist by Dorothy, who dresses in blue velvet herself. The song seems to be her signature song.

During her performance we catch a view of the dreaded Frank Booth (Dennis Hopper), who obviously is mesmerized by her performance. We get the impression that the maniacal Frank is getting more than serene aethetic pleasure from Dorothy's soulful interpretation of the song. We won't need to wait very long to find out just what Frank's connection with Dorothy is.

Meanwhile, Jeffrey has rashly decided to go into Dorothy's apartment in spite of Sandy's protest. "You shouldn't do this," she says. "Why not?" he retorts. This obsessive streak in Jeffrey brings forth her observation: "I don't know if you are a detective or a pervert." "That's for me to know and you to find out," Jeffrey responds childishly.

Jeffrey indulges his curiosity, goes in, and pokes around her apartment. He finds toys but no child. His voyeuristic enjoyment is interrupted when Dorothy arrives home. Sandy, who has been Jeffrey's lookout outside, flees in terror. Jeffrey can't escape so he hides in a clothes closet. His pleasures intensify when he peeks through the door louvers as Dorothy undresses before him.

Unfortunately for him, she discovers him and angrily confronts him with a knife. She threatens to kill him. She makes him disrobe and begins to humiliate him when Frank Booth and his entourage arrive at her door. There is a scramble and Jeffrey returns to his hiding place so that Dorothy can let Frank in.

Booth enters and reveals an absolutely deranged and perverse character. He curses and abuses Dorothy verbally, then demands sexual access. He puts a strip of blue velvet in his mouth, breathes from a canister of gas stimulant that he has brought with him, and attacks her sexually while he calls her "Mommy." He obviously cannot consummate the sexual act in a normal fashion, but is able through these weird means to gain some sort of perverse satisfaction. We gather that this is a ritual that Frank imposes periodically on Dorothy. He leaves as abruptly as he came.

Jeffrey has gotten more than even his curiosity had demanded. He has watched the whole thing in horror. He tries to comfort Dorothy. She at first rejects him but then accepts his tender attention. Oddly enough, she then initiates love-making with this voyeur who has sneaked into her apartment. In the midst of their passionate encounter she alternatively pleads: "Hit me!" and "Help me!"

By now we have an accurate picture of the characters in the movie. Not one of them is normal. Jeffrey is compulsively nosey. Sandy is a silly, superficial ninny. The peripheral characters are robots. Frank Booth and his gang are the epitome of violent perversity. Frank himself is dangerously bestial. His favorite word is "fuck," which he uses to refer to killing or abuse. While it is clear he can "fuck" by killing, it is also evident that he cannot act out the conventional meaning of that term. Furthermore, the plot is moving horrifically downward and the background atmosphere of the movie is malevolent. Nothing bodes well.

Jeffrey deteriorates further by getting more deeply involved with Dorothy. Their sado-masochistic encounters are accompanied by beastly and disgusting sounds. His relationship with Sandy suffers when she senses his mind and body are elsewhere. But he seems unable to extricate himself from the strange allure of Dorothy.

Jeffrey's obsessive curiosity is finally squelched with a terrible ride into hell. Frank catches him at Dorothy's place and sets out to teach him a lesson. He forcibly takes both Dorothy and Jeffrey on a high speed trip into his world, a world of drug addicts, sexual perverts, criminals, and torturers. This world, we find out, is where Dorothy's husband and child are held in hostage by Frank. As long as he holds them, he has the leverage to coerce Dorothy into his kinky sexual activities and to keep her from going to the police.

Jeffrey barely escapes with his life, at least partly due to Dorothy's brave interventions with the deranged Frank. After a night of awful dreams—winds keep blowing out candles—Jeffrey awakes in tears. He has been cured of his undue curiosity and immediately goes to the police with his story. Unfortunately, we have little confidence in the police. Det. Williams, Sandy's dad, still seems like he's in a daze and we find out that one of the detectives under him is in cahoots with Frank Booth.

There is an interlude when Jeffrey and Sandy are reconciled. They dance together to a wonderfully romantic song and pledge their eternal love to each other. No sooner have they have made up than Dorothy appears at Jeffrey's home—confused, abused, and naked. He comforts and embraces her, to the great chagrin of Sandy. But Jeffrey is not shocked or fazed by this horrible scene; he knows that Dorothy has been abused again by Frank and he offers his protection. He is no longer "involved" sexually with Dorothy.

A message from Det. Williams indicates that Dorothy's kidnapped husband has been returned to her apartment. Jeffrey rushes there to find her husband dead along with the crooked detective, who evidently had failed Frank. Both dead men are in grotesque postures. Frank now comes to the apartment to finish off Jeffrey. He appears in a bizarre disguise but armed to the teeth. Jeffrey, unable to escape from the apartment, hides in a closet clutching the gun he has taken from the body of the crooked cop. Frank searches in a maniacal frenzy for Jeffrey. As he approaches the closet, Jeffrey surprises him with a tremendous blast to the chest. The monster is finally felled.

The last scene of the movie finds Jeffrey and Sandy happily married. They are enjoying a picnic with Jeffrey's again-healthy father and his aunts. Dorothy is seen playing with her son at another location. But something doesn't feel right. The lovely flowers are plastic, the policemen act like robots and the peaceful scene seems an illusion. A robin, earlier used as a symbol of love, appears on the garden fence. But on closer view it is chewing a squirming bug, a disgusting sight. Lumberton is again restored to normalcy?

What to make of this gripping but weird film? On one level, the viewer can be angered by the movie. It shocks and titillates, but finally disgusts many viewers by its portrayals of perverse violence. Is the director simply playing with our emotions, giving us a good thrill, but manipulating us at the same time? Some viewers think there is no serious intent at all behind the movie. It is merely example of directors pushing thrills to the extreme edge of acceptability. *Blue Velvet* is a sophisticated *Texas Chain Saw Massacre*.

That it seems to me, underestimates the movie. The continuing attention given it by serious movie-goers suggests something more than cheap thrills. Perhaps it is a Christian film, as David Lynch himself has sometimes hinted. On the surface one could make that claim. Jeffrey, for example, can be viewed as a Christian tragic hero. He begins with a serious internal flaw, the obsessive curiosity that gets him into so much trouble. The plot pushes him from his safe bondage into a pressure point of immense turbulence—his frightening ride into hell. He seems to repent and open his heart to the movement of grace. Further, he manifests a new life, free from past obsessions and free for effective dealings with Sandy, Dorothy, and the onerous challenge provided by Frank Booth.

But can one take this interpretation seriously? At the end of the movie we seem to be back at the beginning. The environment is plastic, the humans robotic, and the robin, symbol of love, is munching a writhing bug. Jeffrey and Sandy seem lobotomized. The atmosphere at the end seems as disturbing as it was at the beginning. The happiness and light are merely a veneer over something truly awful at a deeper level. The atmosphere doesn't allow us to take a Christian interpretation of the story seriously.

The director's attitude (or what we have been calling the tone of the movie) mocks the happy ending as well as the "transformation" of the characters. Neither can be believed, he seems to say. He looks with skepticism on any deep-down redemptive possibility.

Thus, the movie should be understood as basically skeptical. The characters never move beyond a deep weirdness and one expects the plot to start all over with some new malevolence popping up. The churning, chaotic maelstrom below the surface of reality has not disappeared; it is only buried temporarily. It will break out again, perhaps in Jeffrey's and Sandy's superficially conventional lives. Reality and its creatures cannot be trusted. They are frightening at a deeper dimension.

Crimes and Misdemeanors

In this Woody Allen movie, the hero—or better, the anti-hero— literally gets away with murder. The film continues Allen's exploration of religious themes, though a case could be made that this one is the end of the line. Any transcendent reality, with the grounding it might give to objective standards of morality, seems to have been dissolved. There is only "winning" and "losing" according to who has power, cunning, and a bit of luck. Thus, this movie finds the anti-hero winning at the end, in spite of perversity of character and wickedness of deed. Further, he remains sane and "happy."

The story begins with Judah Rosenthal being honored as a philanthropist by an adoring group of friends and associates at a dedication dinner. His wife, Miriam, and his children join in honoring him. He has given money for a new ophthalmology wing of a large hospital. He gives a speech in which he recalls a wise saying by his father: "The eyes of God are always on us." He no longer believes in God, he says, but he remains committed to the ethical values of Judaism—justice and mercy.

Eyes, sight, and light are important symbols in the movie. Judah is an eye doctor, God's eyes are on us, sight allows us to see what is right and good, and light is necessary for eyes and sight to work. One of Judah's patients is his rabbi, Ben, who, unfortunately, is going blind. While the physical side of his sight is declining, he at the same time is a symbol of another kind of sight—spiritual and moral wisdom. Ben is an important conversation partner of Judah.

Judah's righteousness is merely surface, however. He has been having a long affair with Delores Paley, who believes that Judah is going to leave his wife and family for her. Judah intends no such thing, though he has told Delores he will do so. Further, we find out that Delores knows that Judah's wealth has not been honestly gained. He is an embezzler as well as a cheat and liar.

Judah has grown tired of Delores and wants to terminate the relationship. Delores not only continues her love for Judah, but has also staked her future on his promise to marry her. She is determined to fight for him in spite of his desire to end the affair. She demands that Judah, Miriam, and she meet together to thresh things out.

Miriam does not know about the affair and Judah wants badly to maintain the facade of a happy married and family life. Delores's threatened fuss is potentially a great danger to Judah, particularly since she knows of his shady financial dealings, and since she intends to make his relations with her public. Moreover, she has grown wild and hysterical in her threats. Judah knows he cannot control her. He is in a first-class mess.

Judah talks to Ben, the rabbi, about his quandary. Ben encourages Judah to confess his sins to Miriam and plead for forgiveness. He insists there is a moral structure to life that Judah has violated. But, he promises, there is a spark—a conscience—in Judah that commands that he repent, confess, and live a more upright life. Ben represents one horn of the dilemma in which Judah is caught. The religious view of life demands submission to real moral standards.

The other alternative open to Judah is represented by his brother, Jack. Jack has jettisoned his Judaism and lives on the fringes of the criminal underground of the city. He has survived and prospered in the rough and tumble of life. "I know what reality is like," he declares, and in that reality "God is a luxury I can't afford." He resents the way that the conventional world, including Judah, looks down on him.

Nevertheless, as a brother Jack is willing to give Judah some advice and offer help in getting him off the hook. Jack suggests that Judah have Delores murdered and offers to hire a killer to get the job done. Judah is horrified at the suggestion. But Jack offers this rejoinder: "I think you need to play hard-ball." He feels both resentment and satisfaction that he has to do the dirty work for his squeamish and hypocritical brother.

Judah is haunted by his decision to let Jack set up the murder. He hears the voice of Ben saying that without the Law of God all is darkness. But he justifies his deed by telling himself that Delores has done him a serious injustice. He's already convinced himself that he made no promises of marriage to her.

The secret message from Jack that Delores has been killed comes to Judah in the midst of a party. "God have mercy" he says to himself as he hastily leaves the party to go to Delores's apartment where he gingerly steps around her body to fetch the love-letters he has written her. He makes off with the last evidence of his connection with her before the police can find it. A statue of Schubert eyes him accusingly as he makes his way out. A flashback of his father brings an additional reminder that God punishes the wicked.

A series of conversations and flashbacks provide commentary on the struggle going on in Judah's soul. Ben has gone blind and he tells Judah despairingly that "the eyes are the windows of the soul." Ben now seems to be in darkness and no longer offers wisdom to Judah. Judah confesses his anguish about the murder to Jack but Jack brushes him off: "Forget about it—it was either you or her. You only go around once so you have to put yourself first." A flashback to a childhood family dinner brings back a conversation in which a hard-nosed leftist aunt argues with Judah's father. She takes the position that might makes right while he holds out for divine retribution for evil.

Another interesting commentary is interjected in the plot. It consists of a television program featuring a Professor Levi who is making the humanist case for humanly-defined morality and justice. We no longer have the prop of religion to which to cling for the grounding of our morality, he argues. We are alone in the universe, but that does not mean we should despair in our pursuit of a human morality and justice. However, a later news report brings the disturbing announcement that Professor Levi has committed suicide. (The reflections of the professor are those of Primo Levi, an Italian Jewish philosopher who actually did commit suicide.) So much for the human construction of morality. Such humanist hope doesn't turn out to be very hopeful.

Judah still is full of torment, but his life goes on as before. At the end of the movie we find him at the wedding of his daughter. After the conclusion of this happy event he confides his private thoughts directly to us who have viewed his story in the movie. His murder story has a strange twist, he ruminates. After many weeks of guilt provoked by his religious background, he finally faces up to reality as it is. We are the sum total of our choices. There is nothing beyond us to judge us. If we are clever enough we can hide our own misdeeds. With that realization, Judah woke up one morning and the crisis was lifted. The sun was shining. His guilt was gone. He had made it through a difficult time successfully. He got away with murder.

In this skeptical movie the anti-hero wins. Though a wicked scoundrel, he succeeds in extricating himself from the repercussions of his evil deeds. He is unjust but appears just. He has his cake and eats it too. The elements of character, plot, and atmosphere seem to support this skeptical conclusion.

But does the tone of the movie affirm such a person and his way of being in the world? Does Woody Allen approve of Judah? Or is his intention in the movie to make us look straight at a world without external or internal moral structure? Does he intend to make us draw back in horror from such a world and vow to look elsewhere for something more constructive? Or do the movie, and Woody Allen, confirm our worst fears that Jack is the real hero in the movie, the Jack who is willing to act selfishly without concern or remorse? The tone is not conclusive. We are left to decide for ourselves.

Epilogue

We have concluded our depiction of four basic visions of life conveyed in modern movies. The Christian, the American, the Greek, and the skeptical narratives express passionate convictions about the way life really is and the way it ought to be. The elements of narrative—character, plot, atmosphere, and tone—are pulled coherently together into powerful statements about the meaning of our lives. We can see the clear outlines of these visions in many modern films. (Again I add the disclaimer that not all movies are amenable to this kind of analysis.) Such films, though entertaining, are not merely entertainment. They are visions of life.

A final reflection. Do we simply choose which one of these visions is most persuasive to us as individuals? In one important sense the answer to that question is "yes." We are drawn to one or the other by our own experience and interpretation of the world. Sometimes our individual experience and reflection on it leads to an eclectic mixture of these visions. Certainly the individual element cannot be ignored.

But individual interpretations do not occur in a vacuum. We are already bathed in schemes of interpretation that come from our religious, national, and family traditions. These traditions are larger than ourselves and will certainly live beyond us. Some even claim to be the result of divine revelation. If any are really "true," they are true in an objective sense that transcends our own individual interpretations. Moreover, these traditions—these stories—affect the interpretation of our experience as much as our experience confirms or denies the stories.

So there are no easy answers. We struggle to find the truth and hope that the truth finds us. Interpreting serious films may aid us in that search. Ultimately, there is an element of belief that operates in the appropriation of a vision for our lives. But it is not simply "blind" belief that leads us toward a vision, but rather one based on seeing in the deepest sense of the word. Believing we see and seeing we believe.

Appendix A:

Examples of Films by Category

The following is a list of movies categorized according to the different stories we have explored. Some of them fit well with the types of narratives we have delineated but others correspond more loosely. The list is meant to be a helpful guide to those who want to explore serious movies with the approach we have proposed here. It certainly does not include all the movies that could be listed. Many others could be added that may well fit better than the ones I have specified. The viewer is invited to expand the list indefinitely.

The Christian Story

<u>Explicit</u>

Tender Mercies
Babette's Feast
Places in the Heart
Trip to Bountiful
The Mission
Billy Budd
The Fisher King
Sling Blade

Dead Man Walking
Devil's Advocate

Implicit

One Flew Over the Cuckoo's Nest
Five Easy Pieces
The Verdict
Terms of Endearment
Ordinary People
Moonstruck
Requiem for a Heavyweight
Midnight Cowboy
Glory, Glory
Field of Dreams
Nuts
Lone Star

The American Story

The Natural
It's A Wonderful Life
Friendly Persuasion
High Noon
Shane
Rocky
The Searchers
Mr. Smith Goes to Washington
It Happened One Night
The Right Stuff
Stagecoach
Fear Strikes Out
Forrest Gump

The American Nightmare

Easy Rider
Who's Afraid of Virginia Woolf?
Wall Street
Tame the Tiger
Nashville

Network
Cat on a Hot Tin Roof
Long Day's Journey Into Night
Death of a Salesman
The Wild Bunch
River's Edge

The Greek Story

Breaker Morant
The Boat
Gallipoli
The Eagle Has Landed

The Skeptical Story

Easy Rider
River's Edge
Clockwork Orange
Sleuth
The Field
Chinatown
The Inspector Calls
They Shoot Horses, Don't They?
Catch 22
Blue Velvet
Ironweed
Ragtime
Winter Light
Reservoir Dogs
A Handful of Dust
Bonnie and Clyde
Goodfellas
Mean Streets
House of Cards
The Usual Suspects
Natural Born Killers

Appendix B:

On Discussing Films

Interpreting the meaning of films in group discussion can be a daunting challenge. Often the discussion becomes chaotic when persons contribute unrelated points. Other times one person dominates. A typical frustration occurs when the discussion begins with too high a level of abstraction. If a leader tries to order the discussion, it often turns into a lecture.

Helpful exchange of opinion within a group needs to strike a balance between control and freedom, specific information and general interpretation, participation and domination, and between serendipity and intentionality. I have found that using a schedule of questions that moves from the specific to the general and from the descriptive to the interpretative is helpful. With its aid I am sometimes able to strike the balance needed. I offer it here as a guide for the group discussion of films. Approach its use pragmatically; some questions will be found more useful than others.

Pooling Perceptions

The answers, like the questions, should be short and snappy. Debates or long discussions are not helpful at this stage.

1. What were some of the key scenes in the movie?
2. What noises did you notice?
3. Where did you notice music? What kind was it?
4. What colors predominated? Were specific colors related to specific characters?
5. What numbers were used in the film?
6. What symbols did you notice?
7. Name as many characters as possible. Who were the major ones?
8. What important lines do you remember? (Take some time here and write the most important lines on a board or newsprint.)
9. Where did you experience intense emotion? What kind?
10. Where do you remember laughing?
11. What was your mood at the end of the movie?
12. Give one word to sum up the film. (Go around the room.)

Plunging In

1. What characters did you most like? Dislike?
2. With whom did you most identify? Why? (Go around the room.)
3. Did anyone surprise you with their identification? How?

Interpretation

1. What kind of characters do we have in the movie? Bound by sin, determined, noble, or deformed? Analyze the main characters carefully. What are they like at the beginning and at the end?
2. How does the plot proceed? At the beginning, middle, and end? Is its movement characterized best as Christian, American, Greek, or skeptical? Why and how?
3. What happens at the moment of challenge in the middle? How do the main characters respond to the challenge? What happens to them at that point? Repentance and grace, determined overcoming of obstacles, recognition and preparation for doom, or full revelation of their weakness or deformity?
4. How does the movie end? What is the status of the characters? What was your response to their story?
5. How do you interpret the overall meaning of the movie? Can it be helpfully understood in the categories of this book?
6. After you have reflected on the meaning of the movie, has your mood about the film changed?

Endnotes

[1] John R. May, *Image and Likeness: Religious Visions in American Film Classics* (Mahwah, N.J.: Paulist Press, 1992) p. 3.

[2] "The Pictures Inside Our Heads," James Wall, *The Christian Century*, March 18-25, 1992, p. 291.

[3] Rudolf Arnheim, *Film as Art*, (Berkeley: University of California Press, 1957), p.37.

[4] "Film Literacy," *The London Times*, Monday, November 16, 1992, Section 1, p. 19.

[5] T. S. Eliot, "Religion and Literature," in *Essays Ancient and Modern* (New York: Harcourt Brace and World, 1936); cited in *The New Orpheus: Essays toward a Christian Poetic*, ed. Nathan Scott, Jr. (New York: Sheed and Ward, 1964), p. 228.

[6] Michael Medved, *Hollywood vs. America* (San Francisco: HarperCollins, 1992).

[7] Wesley Kort, *Moral Fiber: Character and Belief in Recent American Fiction* (Philadelphia: Fortress Press, 1982) p. 1, and Wesley Kort, *Story, Text and Scripture* (University Park: Pennsylvania State University Press, 1988), p. 18. Kort himself was a student of Preston Roberts, whose essay "A Christian Theory of Dramatic Tragedy," *Journal of Religion*, 31/1, January,

(1951), pp.1-20, provides part of the supporting theory for the approach I am adopting. Kort also relies on theorists such as Gerard Genette, Jean Calloud, and Jonathan Culler, among others.

[8]Kort, *Moral Fiber*, *op.cit.*, p. 2.

[9]I am aware that my approach runs counter to a number of modern theories of interpretation that argue that there is no reliable transpersonal meaning conveyed from the creator of an imaginative work to the viewer or reader. Or at least no such meaning **should** be conveyed. Deconstructionists, for example, argue that claims to objective meaning **should** be debunked. For in their view every work of human imagination is seriously distorted by the interests of the creator. Indeed, from this generally Marxist theoretical perspective, works of art, like economics and politics and social patterns, reflect power relations. The author writes from a particular point of view that must be deconstructed if the reader or viewer is not to be duped by author's construction of the world. Thus, no common, profound, and perennial wisdom about the human condition is conveyed by a work of art, only the partial perspectives of hegemonic interests.

It seems to me that such a perspective is sadly mistaken, as well as professionally self-defeating. It reproduces in the field of literary and film interpretation the crude reductionism that Marxism perpetrated in economic, political, and social analysis. On the contrary, works of art are great because they convey something significant about the human condition that others recognize, not simply because they foist upon us oppressive views of others. Deconstructionism leads too quickly to a kind of epistemological tribalism in which each group has its own truth. At its worst is leaves the discernment of meaning to the solitary viewer or reader alone. Certainly there is more to interpretation than that.

[10]Kort, *Moral Fiber*, p. 5.

[11]Preston Roberts, "A Christian Theory of Dramatic Tragedy," *op. cit.*, p. 12.

[12]I am sorely tempted to use *Babette's Feast* for my account of an explicitly Christian film. This Danish film, which won the 1988 Academy Award for the best foreign film, is a real gem. It is adapted from a story by Isak Dinesen, a story which is not as clearly Christian in its original form as in its movie adaptation. The movie tells the tale of a number of lives that have fallen into despair but who are renewed in a great sacramental feast prepared

by an exiled French master chef, Babette. As in *Tender Mercies*, this film is replete with its own apparatus of Christian commentary. The characters, the accompanying hymns, and the narration all serve to interpret the story as it unfolds. It is an unusually charming and edifying film.

[13]R. W .B. Lewis, *The American Adam: Innocence, Tragedy, and Tradition in the Nineteenth Century* (Chicago: University of Chicago Press, 1955), Perry Miller, *Errand into the Wilderness* (Cambridge: Harvard University Press, 1956), H. R. Niebuhr, *The Kingdom of God in America* (New York: Harper Torchbooks, 1959) and Martin E. Marty, *Righteous Empire: The Protestant Experience in America* (Fort Worth: Dial, 1970).

[14]Robert Benne and Philip Hefner, *Defining America: A Christian Critique of the American Dream* (Philadelphia: Fortress Press, 1974). In this book we try to show in detail the transposition of the Old Testament narrative into the American Dream. The transposition involves archetypal figures like Abraham Lincoln who have lived out the promise of the American Dream. These figures seem to have rootage in the biblical as well as the American story. We go on to show that the American Dream is only a partial expression of the Old Testament vision. Indeed, it accentuates certain values even while it suppresses others. We contend that our national self-understanding is faulty because of this distortion of the biblical narrative.

[15]At the conclusion of the film interpretation course I have been teaching for many years, I conduct a discussion with the students about the movies we have viewed and discussed. Among other things, I ask them which of the dozen or so movies we have viewed is their favorite. To my surprise, *The Natural* has often come out near top. This is a surprise to me because I thought that such a mythic celebration of the American story would be greeted with little enthusiasm by students who have experienced many traumatic challenges to the American Dream. But they enjoy *The Natural* far more than they do the more critical films of the 1960s. My explanatory hypothesis is that the American Dream is far deeper in the American psyche than many have realized. Even when sharp criticism calls into question the optimism of the Dream, American hope persists.

[16]I am aware that there is no single Greek vision. The Greeks, fertile as they were in philosophy and the arts, identified and reflected carefully on many of the possible ways of looking at life. While the Greeks did not deal with the Hebrew vision, they considered most of the philosophical options— idealism, skepticism, materialism, and hedonism, to name a few. Their

analytical ability also enabled them to understand the persisting formal elements in drama, literature, politics, and ethics. The view I am calling "the Greek story" is indebted to the great Greek philosophers—Socrates, Plato and Aristotle—and to the great Greek tragenians—Sophocles and Euripides. Though again there is no simple unity in the perspectives represented by the Greeks just mentioned, there is enough consensus among them to talk of a Greek vision. As I remarked in the preface, I rely on Preston Roberts's analysis of the Greek vision in his seminal essay, "A Christian Theory of Dramatic Tragedy," *op. cit.* Roberts thought there were enough unifying themes to warrant talk about a Greek theory of dramatic tragedy. He argued that that theory was indebted to Greek theology, a typically Greek way of construing the world. I will follow Roberts's view on these matters.

17*Ibid.*, p. 17.

18*Ibid.*, p. 13.